NO PARENT LEFT BEHIND

NO PARENT LEFT BEHIND

HOW TO PARENT TEENS
FROM LOVE INSTEAD OF FEAR

DR. CANDICE FEINBERG

LIONCREST
PUBLISHING

NO PARENT LEFT BEHIND

How to Parent Teens from Love Instead of Fear

ISBN   978-1-5445-1369-0 *Hardcover*

978-1-5445-1368-3 *Paperback*

978-1-5445-1367-6 *Ebook*

This book is dedicated to all of the parents who show up every day to work hard at making the lives of their kids better and emotionally healthier. I am constantly amazed by your willingness to look at the part you play and your desire to be a better parent.

CONTENTS

INTRODUCTION

———

When your child is just a baby, staring up at you with those beautiful, trusting eyes, it's impossible to imagine a day when they'll be slamming doors, sneaking in after curfew, or slouching around the house with a group of questionable friends. It's easy to think that if you just do everything right as a parent, your child will lead the charmed, successful, worry-free life you want for them.

But since you're reading this book, you've probably already realized that even the most angelic babies encounter struggles once they hit the teen years.

For every kid, the struggle looks different. Perhaps your kid's started out looking like standard teenager issues—a depressed and unmotivated attitude, outbursts of anger, over-the-top anxiety about school or social life—but then suddenly escalated into something much more serious.

Maybe you've been doing your son's homework to make sure he doesn't fail out of a class.

Maybe you've been monitoring your daughter's phone and social media messages.

Maybe you've found yourself paying off repeated credit card debt, calling your college student to make sure they wake up for class, or bargaining with the local police to try to keep a drug bust off your kid's record.

Maybe you got a call at work or in the middle of the night that sent your heart into your throat: an overdose, a car crash, a suicide attempt.

No matter what your child's struggle may look like, yours is likely to resemble that of so many other parents who are dealing with the same kinds of issues you are. You're frustrated, exhausted, sad, and, more than anything, scared. The fear you feel for your child, for their health, their safety, and their future, keeps you awake at night.

Your child's struggle may have arisen all of a sudden, but more likely, it's been going on for quite a while—months, or even years. If you think back, you realize the signs were there for a long time. You just didn't see them, or you thought they were a passing thing. Or you hoped that if you didn't pay too much attention to them, they would just go away.

But now you're at the point where you can't deal with it anymore. Not on your own.

And my question for you is, "What took you so long?"

In my experience, the average parent waits two years before seeking out help for their kid's struggle. Two years is a long time, and can be a lot of heartache to go through. As a parent myself, I can understand wanting to do everything you can to help your child. But think about it: if your kid had diabetes, you wouldn't try to treat it on your own for two years before you took them to a doctor.

THE HIDDEN SCRIPT

As parents, we tend to have a script in mind for our child. We believe that if things happen in the right way and in the right order—if all the bits line up—everything will be fine. Following this script makes us feel secure and confident that our kids are going to be safe, happy, and healthy, and that we've done a good job as parents.

As parents, we can ensure that, up to a certain age, our kids follow this script. We decide what they eat for dinner, what time they go to bed, what sports they're going to play, which friends they can spend time with. We have it all planned out: how they're going to go to college (maybe even a certain college), get married (probably to a heterosexual partner), and raise beautiful grandkids (we may even know exactly how many). Yes, the script reflects our love for our kids, but it's also filtered through our individual values.

You may not even know you have these detailed plans in mind until the day your kid goes off-script. Maybe they go off by just a little, or maybe it's by a lot. Either way, they're not on the right path anymore. That is, they're not on *your* path anymore.

As soon as their kids do something that wasn't part of the plan, many parents tumble down a rabbit hole of worst-case outcomes. *My kid won't get out of bed and go to school! She's not going to graduate! She won't get into college! She'll never land a good career!* This fear takes parents to a place where they can't think about anything else. Their whole life is channeled into one thought: *Fix my kid.* They become obsessed with figuring out why the behavior began and trying to contain or control it.

The never-ending quest for "why" can become pretty extreme. A mother once came into my treatment center with a stack of papers about a nutritional supplement she was convinced her son needed. Another mother quit her job so that she could focus full-time on researching and understanding the "why" behind her daughter's issues, and a father told me he was 100 percent sure his daughter's behavior came from wearing thong underwear.

I always tell parents that if you have lung cancer, the treatment is the same whether you got it because you worked in a coal mine or because you smoked. Blame doesn't help solve the problem. The solution lies in moving forward and acting differently.

Fueled by these fears and desperate to prevent their kid from failing, parents end up overcompensating to make up for their kids' underperformance. They start doing their children's homework or completing their college applications. They begin spying on their kids' activities, both online and in real life. In some extreme cases, they might even sleep on their kids' floors, or bribe an athletic coach to get their kid into college. They micromanage their kids' lives, believing that placing fewer demands on them will make it harder for them to fail.

However, this parenting approach has the opposite effect. As soon as a parent gives in, they've effectively lowered the bar for a kid's behavior, which causes harmful behavior to escalate. Even if the parent tries to pull back on what they'll put up with, the pattern of enabling has already gone on so long they don't have the strength to maintain any boundaries. The kid knows that if they push back hard enough or threaten the right things, those boundaries won't be maintained.

Little by little, this dance of dependency becomes standard procedure in the house. Eventually, it reaches a breaking point. This may come in the form of a sudden disaster, or a parent waking up one day and realizing, "My God, when did this become our 'normal'?"

A parent in these straits may spend hours researching their kid's issues on the Internet or seeking advice from friends, but then still hesitate to seek out real help. Believing they can figure it out themselves makes the issue seem not *that* bad. In contrast, reaching out for a qualified resource makes the problem feel like, well, a real problem. As much as a parent may hate and fear their child's negative behavior, they also fear what the behavior says about them as a parent.

A lot of this has to do with the stigma around mental health issues. You don't think of yourself as a bad parent if your kid scrapes their knee or gets chickenpox, right? But so many parents feel that putting their kid in therapy invites judgment. "If I had parented exactly right," they tell themselves, "this wouldn't have happened." Caring for one's mental health is no different from caring for one's physical health. After all, the brain works and grows stronger in the same way that any muscle in your body does. But there remains an unfortunate stigma around seeking professional resources when mental or emotional issues arise.

Underneath the fear associated with seeking professional help, there's an even deeper fear centered around where their kid's behavior could lead. It could be the loss of the child's life or safety; it could be the loss of their promising future; it could be the loss of the parent's relationship with their child. As concerned as the parent is, and as much as they may hate their child's behavior, they may ultimately choose to enable it rather than risk losing them.

That's why by the time a parent reaches out for a book like this one, they are probably in a state of absolute emotional chaos. They've spent years trying to prevent this deep loss that they fear, but they've finally come to a place where they realize that if they don't get help, a loss is going to happen anyway.

GIVING UP CONTROL TO FIND CONNECTION

As a clinical psychologist with over ten years in private practice and running treatment programs for teens with mental health issues, I've seen every unhealthy behavior you can imagine (and a few you can't). I've also seen families change and heal in radical ways. I'm not exaggerating when I say that 100 percent of my clients report improvement in their relationship with their kids. But this doesn't happen by accident. Success depends on parents committing to make the changes that are asked of them and discovering how to connect with their kids.

Connection is truly the missing key in parenting today. It's also a word that gets tossed around a lot, and it's often taken to mean a feeling or emotional state. However, connection is not so much a feeling as a skill you have to learn and practice. It requires removing barriers of fear between your kid and you. Connection is about listening to your kid, allowing them to learn and grow independently, with the goal of launching them into the world.

Fear-based parenting, which, again, prioritizes ensuring your kid follows a "script" over helping them find their own way, values control over connection. When I help parents really dig deep into why they parent from fear, they often discover that it arises out of a reluctance to have their kids not need them as much as they used to.

As kids get older, they naturally start to pull away from their parents. This is a part of forming their own identity, figuring out where they fit in the world. While parental influence will always be a huge part of that, peer influence starts to play a bigger role. Kids start considering ideas they didn't learn at home: becoming vegan, joining the Peace Corps, getting a tattoo.

Even if yours is the closest, happiest family in the world, by a certain time, your kid is going to need some space from you. They're also going to try to engage you in arguments and ruffle your feathers with the things they do and say. This is all part of their growth process. They are learning to make decisions for themselves, question authority, and reason in the abstract. Naturally, they are going to try out these new skills on you—their parent.

When you're parenting out of fear, you miss out on opportunities to gain insight into what's really happening with your kid. Reacting to their behavior by trying to regain control to prevent what you see as catastrophe coming down the road ends up causing conflict and alienation. This is true even when you try not to show your fear, outrage, or disappointment. Kids are incredibly good at picking up any signal of disapproval from their parents. I've heard parents insist, "I never said anything to them about X," and I've responded, "You probably didn't have to." Even if you and your kid have never had a talk about marijuana, college, or same-sex relationships, they know exactly how you feel about those issues and whether they can expect you to listen to them and try to understand if their ideas differ from yours.

Bottom line: connection always stops when fear takes over.

When parents come to the treatment program I run, they're typically asking me and my team to help their kids. But what we end up giving them is an approach to helping themselves. If you've remained focused on "fixing" your kid, ask yourself: Is this working? If the answer is no, that means you have to work on *you*.

Changing a fear-based parenting approach doesn't happen overnight. When parents come to us, they learn how to take a hard look at their own behavior and address their weaknesses, both in parenting and in personal coping skills. They learn to develop the strength they need to resist their children's methods of emotional manipulation and fighting back, and they learn the importance of maintaining a unified front so that there isn't a weak link in the family system their children can exploit to turn them against each other. Parents also learn about what's appropriate behavior to expect from their children at certain ages and how to avoid imposing their values on them. Most importantly, parents learn how to reestablish connection with their children through listening and understanding.

THERE IS HOPE—I PROMISE

If you're in a place where your kid is struggling, you've tried everything, and everything is only getting worse, I promise there is hope for both of you.

Adolescence is a period every kid has to go through. It's rough, exhausting, and confusing, but ultimately, the majority of kids come out of it just fine. As a parent, it's important to remember that while you can prevent a lot of unnecessary turmoil by getting them help when they need it and by changing some aspects of your parenting, ultimately, your kid will find their way. As my dad always used to say, "You turned out all right in spite of me."

It's also important to remember that you did not cause your child's behavioral issues by making some major parenting mistake. Whatever your kid has gone through, and whatever you feel you did "wrong" and now regret, you're not the only one who has ended up where you are. Plenty of other parents have made the same mistakes and their kids don't have the same issues. Actually, plenty of parents have done much worse and their kids are doing just fine. The reality is, each of us is responsible for how we respond to even the most unfortunate events of our lives. And that includes your kid.

This is the kind of thing that most therapists would never say to their clients out of a fear of offending or angering them. I've experienced clients reacting with anger, shock, and displeasure at the things I've told them. But I've remained committed to being honest and doing all I can to help because I know that it's the only way my clients are going to get better.

IT'S NOT TOO LATE TO HAVE THE LOVE YOU WANT

Parenting begins with an incredible feeling of connection. That new baby fits perfectly in your arms, smells good, and looks up at you with utter trust and dependence. Your child wants to be with you all the time, and your whole life revolves around taking care of all their needs. While you may have moments of anxiety or doubt, you know that you'd do anything it takes to keep your child safe, healthy, and happy.

I want you to know that you can get back to that place. Your kids don't need you in the same way they used to, but they do still need to feel connected to you. This book will give you the tools you need to connect with your kids where they are now, to stop the insanity, and to restore your child's chances for a bright future. Your kid's life may not turn out the way you had imagined when you wrote the "script" for it, but you can get back to the place where you can parent out of love and enjoy a relationship with them. They're going to be happy again, and you are, too.

Take a deep breath. It's going to be okay.

CHAPTER ONE

PARENTING FROM FEAR

———

Having raised two boys through teenage years to adult-hood, I've had my moments of crazy just like any other parent. One of the most memorable episodes happened when my oldest son, who is now twenty-five, was in high school.

One of his buddies had a family home on the Sunshine Coast near Vancouver, and this buddy had invited my son and a group of friends from their senior class to come up for a week-long stay.

I'd actually been to this house the previous summer. It's a beautiful little cabin built beside a remote lagoon. You can't reach it by road. Instead, you have to take a seaplane to the dock. There is no nearby town, and only a couple of neighbors. To get around this isolated area, you can either take a boat (in dubious mechanical condition) or an off-road golf cart. During my visit, I'd opted for the latter, only to get out of the cart three times because my son's friend was—how do I put this?—driving like a teenager.

While I definitely liked this friend of my son's, I also knew he was one of those "no fear" kids. He wasn't malicious or a troublemaker. He just had no hesitation when it came to taking risks. This made sense, given that he'd survived leukemia earlier in his life. Another result of this amazing survival was that ever since he'd been diagnosed, his father hadn't been able to say "no" to him.

Of course, the last thing I wanted was to prevent my son from enjoying this final trip with his high school buddies, so I gave him permission to go up to Vancouver for the week. But almost from the moment they left, my head filled up with every conceivable image of danger. Shoddy boats springing leaks. Golf carts careening over a cliff. A slip of the finger while shooting clay pigeons.

I tried to wait a decent number of hours before calling to check on my son. But when he didn't pick up (not the first time, not the second time, not the third time), I began to mentally spiral.

What if they were out on the boat and drinking, and they flipped over and drowned and no one found them?!

What if they were fishing and left fish on the dock, and a bear came out of the woods, and they heard the noise and went outside to see what it was and the bear ate them?!

As a psychologist, I knew I should stop catastrophizing. But as a mom, I just couldn't help myself. For two days, I had so much anxiety I could feel my arms tingling like pins and needles. And since no one was checking on my son and his friends, there was no way for me to find out if they were even alive from one day to the next.

I'll cut to the chase: my son *was* alive and totally fine. He managed to call me back a couple of days later and reported that everything was going just great. I had nothing to worry about.

When I picked him up at the airport at the end of the week, my son had a white gauze bandage wrapped around his calf. I felt a grim satisfaction—my parental instincts had been correct. There *had been* an accident.

He got in the car, and I pointed at the bandage. "What happened?" I asked.

He grinned. "I burnt my leg on a marshmallow skewer when we were making s'mores."

Right. Of course. A marshmallow skewer.

I'd spent a week straight envisioning him sinking a boat or being eaten by a bear, but at no point did I wonder whether he might burn himself. I was too obsessed with the dangers I'd seen during my visit there—the golf-cart driving, the clay pigeon shooting—to consider the great danger of making s'mores.

Turns out, you can't protect someone from the future, especially by worrying about it. No matter how good your imagination might be, the unknown is never what you think.

PARENTING FROM FEAR IN CLINICAL PRACTICE

When parents worry, they are almost never drawing on the facts of situations. Instead, they're drawing on their own experiences and the anxieties associated with them. The fact that I'd actually seen this house in Vancouver gave me plenty of detailed fodder for fear. Interestingly, my son had actually visited this house with just his friend and his friend's dad a year before I did, and I'd had no worries about the visit at that time. I only started to worry once I'd been there myself and formed an image of the dangers.

But just try telling a parent their fears aren't based in a rational assessment of the facts. As someone who does this as a regular part of their job, I can tell you that it doesn't go over well. It's almost as though parents are looking for reasons to worry on behalf of their kids.

I've seen these parental fears manifest in two ways:

#1—BEING AFRAID *FOR* THEIR KID

We love our kids so much. We want everything for them. Nothing can hurt or scare us more than the idea of them being in peril, whether it's their physical safety or their future security that's threatened.

Today's world seems to present all kinds of dangers. Along with the old standby dangers of car crashes, alcohol poisoning, and sports-related injuries, today's parents are confronted by dangers that they themselves never could have imagined as children. One of my current patients is a teenage girl addicted to Google chatrooms, where she has met and interacted with a series of older men. This girl's mom is terrified her daughter will be lured out to meet one of these men in person, raped, and even kidnapped. (This mother is not necessarily wrong to be worried about this!)

Sometimes a parent's fear arises because a child has already engaged in self-destructive behavior. Once that fear manifests, it's hard for parents to let it go. They think, "He tried to commit suicide once. He could do it again," and their instinctive response is to start sleeping on his floor in order to keep him safe. They also permit their children to engage in unhealthy behaviors, as long it's under their own supervision. I have parents who rationalize letting their kid play video games all day in their room or smoke marijuana in the house, saying, "At least I know where he is. He's not out getting into trouble."

Being afraid for your child doesn't always involve a physical threat. One teenaged patient of mine had a lot of conflict with the other boys on his water polo team. As a result, he quit the team just before they qualified to play in the Junior Olympics. The patient's mom was beside herself with fear. She saw her son's decision as deliberately throwing away his future. All his former teammates would pass him by, getting into good schools and even getting scholarships. How would his life turn out by comparison?

On the other hand, parents sometimes are afraid of their child's success, because it could lead to failure later. They feel more comfortable keeping their kid dependent on them, so they parent in such a way as to limit their child's choices or personal motivation. I know a mom whose daughter is dragging her feet on college applications. While she says that she wants to go away to college, she's in her senior year and still hasn't started applying. But here's the twist: the mom doesn't think her daughter is *ready* to go away. I had to ask the mother, "Are you not placing demands on your daughter because you don't want to be pushy, or because you don't actually want her to go?"

Fear that their children will fail leads parents to micromanage their kids' lives, doing all their problem-solving for them. But by living under a cloud of constant impending doom, parents can become obsessive. For example, when I ask teenagers with eating disorders how much of their headspace is taken up by food, most say 80 percent. When I ask their parents how much headspace goes into planning their child's life, parents report the same percentage. These parents believe that if they let go, the worst will happen.

#2—BEING AFRAID *OF* THEIR KID

There is nothing more personal than the parent-child relationship. Because of that, as parents, we're already a little afraid of our kids before they are even born. While we're afraid of losing our kids to some sort of outside harm, we're equally afraid of simply losing their love.

Many parents fear they'll never be forgiven if they push their kids into treatment. They also fear reprisal, and teenagers are absolute geniuses when it comes to finding their parents' most sensitive vulnerabilities. (When my son was fifteen, he yelled at me during a fight, "You're never going to see your grandkids." Oooh, did that one ever hurt—he knew how much I love babies.)

I've heard kids lob the following threat at parents who deeply value education: "If I go to treatment, I'm going to fall behind in school." Some kids will even threaten parents with escalation of the same behavior that got them into treatment in the first place. For example, they'll warn their parents that it's dangerous for them to be around other kids in treatment programs. I've had parents call me and say, "I hear there's a kid in the program who uses hard drugs. My kid's not *that* bad—I don't want him to start acting like that other kid." (I have to assure them that behavior isn't contagious like the chickenpox.) A mom once told me her son was adamantly opposed to treatment because we wouldn't allow him internet access. If he didn't have the internet, he warned, he'd get so depressed he'd probably kill himself. I said, "Okay, but where does this end? If he says he's going to kill himself if you don't buy him a BMW, are you going to do that too?"

Often, what parents don't realize is that the minute they give in to fear, they lose their ability to parent.

WHY PARENTING FROM FEAR STARTS IN THE TEEN YEARS

We're wired to care for our kids, but at some point, we can reach a place where we can no longer tell the difference between fear and love.

Adolescence is usually when this special type of dysfunction begins. From age seven to eleven, kids are in a pretty static phase of development—a time that Freud called "latency." During this time, they grow physically and learn a lot, but they don't undergo very significant changes. This means parents can be totally in control without even trying that hard. When your kids are in this age range, they look up to you; they want your attention and approval. Everything goes exactly according to plan.

But then the developmental shift of puberty kicks in. Suddenly, kids have new cognitive skills in their minds, not to mention a surge of hormones running through their bodies. They also become more argumentative, not necessarily because they're angrier, but because they're learning to think for themselves. At the same time, they're more emotional. They also feel the need to try out possible identities—they want to protest, become vegetarians, get tattoos, join the Peace Corps. In their quest to define themselves, kids push parents away despite still needing them.

This is all part of becoming independent. But this shift can be so rapid that it creates parent-child conflict. Giving adolescents the freedom they crave means losing some measure of control over them. All you can do is watch your kid try out their wings and hope they still have their roots. It's a challenging time for parents. For some, it's more than they can handle.

One girl I know told her mom she was going to meet a boy at the mall. It wasn't even a date—the girl and boy were just friends—but her mom couldn't deal with it. She said, "It's fine if you go, as long as I can walk fifty feet behind you."

I had to ask this mom, "What do you think they're going to do at the mall?" From what I could see, there was no danger in this meet-up. But the mom's response communicated one thing loud and clear to her daughter: that her mom didn't trust her.

Not trusting your kids teaches them that the world is a very dangerous place. This belief holds them back from moving forward toward adulthood in even the most basic ways.

For example, I've noticed that fewer and fewer kids in Southern California apply for their driver's license at sixteen. When I was young, I couldn't wait to get my license—I lined up to take my driving test on my sixteenth birthday. But kids today are shying away from this crucial life skill, along with many others.

Another example is the trend of adult children living at home. Pew Research data shows that there are more 18- to 35-year-olds living at home with their parents today than there have been in over a hundred years.[1] The world is objectively less dangerous today than it was even a generation ago—there is less crime today than when I was a kid[2]—yet parents are teaching their teens by example that the world is a scary place full of challenges they're unable to cope with. These parents' fears have fostered a dependence their teens can't break away from.

So how do parents fall into this pattern in the first place?

TEENS ARE SCARY

There's no getting around the fact that stakes are higher once you're parenting teenagers. When a kid is ten years old, you might worry about them climbing too high up a tree, falling, and breaking a bone. But when the same kid is sixteen, you start to worry that they will drive too

---

1   http://www.pewresearch.org/fact-tank/2017/05/05/
    its-becoming-more-common-for-young-adults-to-live-at-home-and-for-longer-stretches/

2   Violent crime has decreased every year since 1994 and yet most Americas think there is more
    crime than ever. https://www.brennancenter.org/blog/americas-faulty-perception-crime-rates

fast and wrap their car around a tree. The teenage years mean the worst-case scenarios get a lot worse.

For many parents, their go-to way of reckoning with these higher stakes is micromanaging. They think they're being controlling out of love; however, there's a reason behind the saying, "Only a mother can love her kid to death."

Remember the girl I mentioned earlier, who was talking to older men in chat rooms? During one group therapy session, her mom made the decision her daughter shouldn't have a phone, iPad, or any other Internet communication device. But at our very next session, this girl showed up with a laptop computer in her bag. When I asked about it, her mom said the computer was necessary for school.

I said, "Okay, but she's not at school right now. Why are you letting her carry it around with her?"

The mom's reply? "The only way I know what she's up to is by her having some type of device."

The mom was actually tracking her daughter's activity on the computer to the extent that she was even reading her daughter's online journals. The mom was exposing her daughter to risk just to keep control...or a sense of it, anyway.

The most fear-based parent behaviors I've seen are in response to children's past behaviors. If a kid has already done drugs or ended up in the hospital from depression or anxiety, the parents are much more afraid. I know a couple that not only refuses to ever leave their kid alone at home, but takes turns sleeping on the floor of his room. These parents think their restrictiveness is keeping their child safe, but it's actually enabling the kid's self-harming behavior by fostering dependence. With no independence at all, the kid lost access to his social circle and leaned on his parents for all his emotional needs.

All the development that happens during the teen years brings yet another delightful surprise: mental health problems that may have been lying below the surface. When a kid is three or five, it's easy to think back on a hard time or traumatic incident in your child's life and think, "Yeah, that was a bad time, but he got through it just fine." In reality, however, many emotional consequences of traumatic experiences are delayed until the brain develops enough to process them. For many kids, age thirteen is the magic number that brings the damage from emotional and mental trauma to light.

If a child experienced an abandonment—even an unintentional one, such as a parent's stint in rehab or the hospital—that experience lasts for life. That child can grow up and become quite successful, only to experience the aftershocks of abandonment at age fifty or later.

One story that illustrates this comes from the great psychiatrist, Gabor Mate. In his book, *In the Realm of Hungry Ghosts*, he tells the story of growing up in Budapest in the 1930s, when the country was newly fascist, posing a major threat to his Jewish family. To save his life, his mother gave him to her neighbor for protection. Fast-forward seventy years, and Mate is on a plane, coming home after a work trip. Once the plane lands at the airport, he gets a text message from his wife, saying, "You're going to have to take an Uber home. I can't pick you up." His first reaction was hurt, rage, vengeance: "That bitch! I'm going to leave her," he thought. But in a few moments, he realized his reaction had nothing to do with his wife not picking him up from the airport. Instead, his reaction stemmed from feeling abandoned by his mother when she gave him away. In other words, he was carrying trauma from a good and necessary parenting decision his mother made to save his life.

Decisions are sometimes forced on parents by circumstances beyond anyone's control, from political catastrophes to natural disasters and so much more. Abandonment issues like Gabor Mate's can result from something as simple as a new sibling being born. For a time, oldest children have their parents to themselves.

When the next baby is born, they suffer a real loss. But just because the loss is real doesn't mean that the parents were wrong to have another child.

The point is that perfectly fine parenting decisions or even acts of heroism like that of Mate's mother can still leave scars. We want to be perfect parents, but it's not always possible.

This brings us to the second reason for parenting out of fear:

PARENTING IS SCARY

When a couple is expecting, they don't say, "You know what? Let's really mess this kid up." We all set out to be better parents than we had. We say with the best intentions, "I'm never going to do the thing that my mother/father did." However, we only have our own limited experiences to draw from. Because we're working out of our own memories and projections, we usually don't even realize when we're doing something hurtful to our kids. How could we? We only know what hurt *us*, not what will hurt them.

This is not a new problem. In fact, even Socrates talked about it. In one of Plato's dialogues, Socrates and his student Phaedrus are discussing rhetoric. Phaedrus is excited about the possibilities of written language, which was still a new and exciting idea at the time. Socrates more or less said, "No. Writing is going to be horrible. We won't talk to each other anymore." He thought that any change to the way people communicated could only be for the worse.

For thousands of years that have come and gone since then, it seems as though every advance in communication has been met with rejection and fear. When the telegraph was invented, customs officers destroyed its prototype because they thought the machine would be used for spying. Today, parents are terrified of the Internet—not just of the many dangerous opportunities it offers, but of the medium itself. That's why we constantly ask ourselves, "Is the Internet addictive?"

> The only technology that caused a real, demonstrable impact on socialization was the television. Unlike the telephone or the Internet, both of which still allowed for socialization, the TV was a one-way medium that stopped people from leaving their houses.

In its essence, the Internet is a medium of functional behavior, just like reading or making a phone call or writing a letter. Using the Internet is necessary now for getting a job, going to college, and performing any number of other basic adult tasks.

At the same time, of course, the Internet can be used to pursue harmful and addictive behaviors. The behaviors are the problem, not the Internet itself. However, if something is already on your mind, you'll see more of it everywhere you look.

My family doesn't eat a lot of fast food. I wasn't raised with it; neither were my kids. One time, I had someone else's kid in the car while I was driving down the main boulevard in town. He looked out the window and said, "Oh, there's a McDonald's on this street." Despite having driven down that street a million times, I'd never known that there was a McDonald's there. I'd noticed the juice shop, the florist, the plumbing supply shop—the things I was interested in. This kid was interested in fast food, so that's what he saw.

The problem isn't that the world is scary. It's that your *kid* is scary because they're attracted to things that aren't good for them. When parents say to me, "My child was never interested in smoking weed until they started hanging around these new friends," I remind them that their kid chose those friends in the first place. When they say the Internet seduced their kid into talking with online predators, or that having a smartphone influenced their kid to post nude photos, I remind them that not all kids do that as a result of using the Internet or smartphones. We only believe that these behaviors are normal because they have become *our* normal.

HOW PARENTING FROM FEAR SHOWS UP IN BEHAVIOR

We've already talked about how fear begets a tendency for parents to control and micromanage. Everything's going normally when all of a sudden, your newly teenaged kid does or says something to inspire fear in your heart. Maybe you find a vape in her pocket. Maybe her grades start to drop. Maybe you overhear her throwing up in the bathroom after dinner. Maybe she starts hanging around with a group of kids you don't like.

The fear these behaviors inspire in a parent leads to one of the three responses we're all familiar with:

FIGHT

Imagine driving down the fast lane and seeing a car coming head-on toward you. Your fear kicks in. Your body goes into sympathetic arousal, a state in which survival mechanisms are heightened. Blood rushes to your core to protect your vital organs. All nonessential functions are deprioritized. Your digestion slows down. Your ability to use language becomes impaired. Your rational mind takes a backseat to pure instinct.

You've probably experienced all of these highly physical fear responses at some point in your life as a parent. Maybe it was when you got that call from the school, the note from the neighbor, the visit from the police. As parents, we experience fear for our kids even more intensely than we experience it for ourselves. When I worried my son was being eaten by a bear in the woods outside Vancouver, I could feel my body getting ready for a fight. That's why my arms were tingling, while in the meantime, my brain was shutting down all rational thought, making me unable to restrain my own crazy behavior.

When something very bad happens, such as when a child attempts suicide and ends up in the hospital, the parent brain can go into overdrive. Without a second thought, parents jump up to fight for their child's survival. They remove all medications and sharp objects from the house. They call the kid's teachers, their coaches, and even their friends in an attempt to enlist support or to investigate the causes of their child's behavior. Parents may even dive into the Internet for answers. I had one mom show up for her son's therapy session with a file folder full of printouts from WebMD and other health and wellness sites. Holding up the folder as proof that she'd thoroughly researched the Internet for what caused teen suicide, and it had given her the answer: a gluten allergy. This, she insisted, explained everything about her son's depression and self-harming tendencies. Meanwhile, I was sitting there thinking about how her kid had presented zero symptoms of gluten intolerance while wolfing down a pizza during our counseling session the day before.

We want to fix the problem so badly, but we're so emotionally connected to it that we can't think logically about it. In trying to figure out why a bad thing happened, all sense of perspective goes out the window. The real irony is that it ultimately doesn't matter why it happened. The "why" is the least important thing a parent needs to figure out during a time when their child is in crisis.

FLIGHT

The "flight" response in parenting usually translates to enabling a kid's behavior by putting up no resistance. For example, if a kid is depressed and seems likely to hurt himself, parents respond by taking him shopping or buying him ice cream. It's action, but it's not productive action. It gradually turns into placing fewer and fewer demands on the kid, so as not to stress him out. The longer this enabling goes on, the more it spreads to other areas, changing the entire family dynamic. By the time parents realize how much their dynamic has changed, they're doing everything for the kid—bringing him breakfast, coaxing him out of bed, helping him choose clothes for the day, driving him to school, doing his homework for him. And in most cases, the kid just lets them. Wouldn't you, if someone was doing everything for you?

Even as this enabling pattern goes on, parents become more frustrated in direct proportion to their fear. This can create a pattern of wildly swinging between those two emotional extremes, a pattern that does not lead to good boundaries. When frustration wins out, parents become too restrictive. Then, out of fear-fueled remorse, they become way too lenient. I'll never forget the dad who made his daughter smash her phone with a hammer one day only to buy her a brand new phone the next day.

FREEZE

In the face of danger to their child, some parents respond by shutting down altogether. They notice that something is wrong, but they ignore it. When they open the door to their kid's room and see it's a mess, they just close it. If they find a lighter in their kid's pocket, they'll just throw it away. If they see or overhear something in a kid's messages or phone calls, they'll resolve to never eavesdrop again, because they don't want to know what's going on. When there's a cut on their kid's arm, they don't ask the kid what's going on. Parents in that place of fear don't want to know more.

It's not that they're oblivious or uncaring. It's that the anxiety and fear is so overwhelming that their brains just shut it out. They protect themselves with fantasy or justification. Maybe it was a one-time deal and will never happen again. Maybe they misunderstood—it was someone else's joint in the kid's pocket. They tell themselves, "My kid's doing fine, this is all normal teenager stuff." They treat each problem like an isolated incident, until it all becomes too much. When they finally admit something is wrong and rewind the tape, they think, "Oh my God. It was there all along. Why did I let it get this far?"

WHY I ADVISE AGAINST PARENTING FROM FEAR

As a parent, I understand that the fear you experience is real. There are legitimate reasons to worry about your child's health, safety, and security. Self-harming, doing drugs, or having trouble in life are real threats. The problem is that, though your fears are real, acting on them does not lead to effective solutions. All it does is create dependent teens and codependent adults.

CODEPENDENCY

I'M OK iF YOU ARE LEARNiNG TO...

STAY iN YOUR LANE

Julie Lythcott-Haims, a former admissions officer for Stanford, gave a TED Talk[3] that I constantly refer to in my work with kids and their parents. In it, she drew attention to the number of students whose parents are still monitoring their movements, even in college. A father once called Lythcott-Haims in her office to ask, "Can you go check on my kid? I haven't heard from him, and I'm worried."

---

3   https://www.ted.com/talks/
      julie_lythcott_haims_how_to_raise_successful_kids_without_over_parenting?language=en

Concerned for the student's safety, she said, "Sure. I'll send someone over to the room to see if he's there."

"Oh, he's there," said the dad. "I can see the tracker dot on my phone."

Confused, Lythcott-Haims asked how long it had been since the father had heard from his son. "A day and a half," was the father's answer.

This talk drew attention to the problem of helicopter parenting. At the point when we're calling our college-age kids to make sure they wake up for class, getting our high schoolers tested for conditions that could give them extra time for the SAT's or ordering for our middle schoolers in restaurants, we're not raising independent adults.

This dependency starts long before the teen years. The classic example is a mom trying to get out of the house in a hurry while her kid struggles to tie his shoes. Tired of waiting, she leans down and does it for the child. Another example is a dad giving his kid a broom and asking her to help sweep the floor. The child makes a few swipes and begins to complain, so the dad rolls his eyes, takes the broom and sends her off to play—the chore will get done faster, without any whining, if he just does it himself.

Both actions might seem innocuous. But in both cases,

what the parent is actually doing is telling the child, "You're not capable." This creates an insecurity that lasts for years, long after the child finally masters tying his shoes. By doing something for the child that he is able to do for himself (even if it does take longer and more effort), the parent has robbed the child not only of an important life skill, but worse, of an opportunity to gain self-confidence.

Some therapists still tell me they are "working on self-esteem" with their teen clients. But there's no treatment manual for self-esteem. Self-esteem isn't a skill; it's a by-product of using your other skills to make good choices.

When we're moving toward what we value instead of away from it, we feel good about ourselves. If we value physical fitness, choosing to go to the gym feels good, even if we hate every minute we spend there. We don't have to *like* our choices, but we do need to make choices that align with our values.

If a mom ties her kid's shoes, what happens next? The next time, the kid will say, "Can you do it for me?" He's already been corrected, so he feels insecure. He doesn't know that he's participating in a situation of dependency—he just knows that he feels better when mom does it.

And let's be honest: much of the time, we parents would

rather be needed than have our kid learn to be independent. Along with making children dependent, parenting from fear makes parents codependent.

When I check in with the parents of my teenage patients and ask how they're doing, it's very common for them to say things like, "I'll be okay once my kid is okay." As a parent, you can probably relate to that feeling. However, this statement is a huge red flag for codependency. Wrapping your happiness or sense of identity up in the success or failure of your child will significantly erode your ability to parent effectively. Codependency cancels out any ability you might have to give your struggling teen the help they need.

I completely understand the feeling of not being able to be happy while your kid is struggling or in danger. It's not always easy to find the line between letting your kid face their own consequences and exposing them to life-threatening danger—between protecting them and enabling them.

One of my teenage patients routinely sneaked out of the house to go and buy drugs. Her mother found out about it and, understandably, freaked out. But rather than assert a boundary, the mother ended up offering to drive her to the drug dealer's house. It was, after all, in a bad part of town. By driving, the mother reasoned, at least she'd be with her and could keep her safe.

I don't expect parents to make rational decisions when they fear for their child's life. That's why it's so important to access outside help. Parents believe they have to do what they're doing, because they love their kid; they seldom realize they're causing a problem. They need to hear from someone who isn't as emotionally invested.

I tend to meet parents at their breaking point, when they've finally admitted, "I can't do this on my own anymore." But the truth is that they never could. They knew, at some level, that their kid was sick. They knew they had to take her to the doctor. But because of the stigma around mental health, getting help for their kid took much longer than it should have.

It's so sad to see the looks of defeat and hopelessness on these parents' faces, especially because this so unnecessary. Everyone has a mind as well as a body, which means there shouldn't be a stigma around mental health any more than there's a stigma around physical health. It should be normal to take whatever measures are needed to get our minds as well as our bodies in good shape and help them recover from sickness or injury. Imagine how much happier our society would be if everyone went in for a therapy checkup each year, just as they go in for a physical checkup.

Just like the body, the brain compensates for untreated

injuries. When you suffer a broken toe, your entire gait will change to compensate. This adjusted gait prevents some of the pain and inconvenience, but it will really mess up your muscles and tendons over time. Even after your toe recovers, you can end up with hip or back problems. It happens gradually, so that you don't notice it until a breakdown "suddenly" occurs.

Mental breakdown works the same way. When we go through hard times, our brains shift in complex ways. Instead of taking the time to truly heal, we rewire ourselves to compensate for the grief. Instead of putting our mended hearts back together, we just prevent future hurts. This is a Band-Aid solution—it makes the symptoms a little easier to deal with, but it doesn't heal the wound. Just as a broken toe can cause back problems, a broken heart can damage the quality of our relationships.

THE WAY OUT

When we do things for our kids that they can do for themselves (and I've done this far too many times), we aren't teaching them the skills they need. Kids must learn to tolerate their feelings and pain in healthy ways. They need to fight their own battles.

This is the first great advantage of parenting from love—it teaches kids about natural consequences. If a kid doesn't get his homework done, he gets a worse grade. If a kid forgets her lunch, she'll be hungry. By letting them deal with the consequences of their own behavior, we're telling them they can handle negative situations. We're letting them know they can overcome challenges. We're demonstrating we trust them to make changes to avoid consequences they don't want. As hard as it can be, parenting from love is the most empowering message we can send our children.

CHAPTER TWO

CHILD-REARING WITH LOVE

—

When I was in grade school, my teacher sent each student home with a box of chocolate bars to sell for a class fundraiser. I was excited by the responsibility of it—I even loved breaking down the cardboard box to make the little handles that turned it into a "candy briefcase" I could carry from door to door.

However, I hadn't counted on the market I'd be dealing with. In the apartment complex where I lived, most of the community didn't have a lot of money to spare (my family included). As I walked around trying to sell the candy, I had a lot of interest from neighbors' kids, but most of them couldn't get a dollar or two from their parents to buy from me.

To me, it only made sense to bargain. "Well, what do you

have?" Some had a quarter, some had sixty-five cents. Whatever they could pay, I gave them a bar. With this system, it didn't take long to get rid of all my candy. Feeling very accomplished, I took the envelope of money back to school the next day and turned it in to the teacher. I'd done my part for the fundraiser.

A day or two later, I was playing outside with my friends when my dad stormed up to me. He grabbed me by the arm, dragged me back home, and laid into me: "What did you do?" he yelled. "I had to write a check to the school for thirty dollars!" It turned out that the teacher had called him about the financial discrepancy in my fundraiser envelope and said it was our responsibility to make up the difference.

I explained what I'd done. Oddly enough, it didn't make as much sense to my dad. He was adamant that I work off every cent of the money he'd had to pay. (I bet if I called him right now, he'd still remember the exact amount.)

Looking back, I can't say my dad handled that situation in the best way. He had a habit of overstepping to make his point. I remember another time when he walked into my bedroom and, surveying the mess, picked up a vinyl record off the floor and snapped it in half in his hands. Brandishing the broken pieces, he said to me, "This would have happened anyway—it was on the floor and you'd have stepped on it. Clean your room."

While I can't say that I adopted my dad's parenting style, he taught me the kind of lessons that few kids today receive. This is even true of my kids, if I'm honest. If I'd been the adult in the candy bar situation, I'd have praised my kid for being thoughtful and generous, and never once brought up financial responsibility. But the truth was that thirty dollars was a lot of money for my family at that time, and it was a lesson I needed to learn.

Parents don't often teach lessons anymore, because they don't want their kids to suffer. This applies to even the most basic elements of parenting. For instance, it's rare to meet a parent who makes their kid clean their room anymore. Most parents today see the messy room and just shut the door, while some even go in and clean it themselves. I've done this myself, realizing only later that my desire to save my child from pain isn't the same as loving them. In fact, it's actually hurting them.

WHERE DO YOUR DECISIONS REALLY COME FROM?

In my practice, I hear parents saying things like this all day:

"She shouldn't have to go through what I went through."

"I don't want him to struggle as much as I did."

"I don't want my kids to shoulder that financial burden. They shouldn't have to start from nothing, like I did."

They frame it so nobly, but it's not truly coming from a place of love. Instead, it's coming from a place of fear. Parents think they're protecting their children, but they're actually setting them up to fail.

The past generation's style of parenting focused more on teaching lessons. There was a general understanding that without facing hardships, kids don't learn any skills. In contrast, today's style of parenting creates entitlement and unrealistic expectations. If kids aren't expected to do anything, where can they build their self-esteem and self-efficacy? Without learning to withstand suffering, kids can't function in life, because life includes suffering.

When my son was a kid, he had a pacifier. Every so often, either my husband or I would say, "I'm throwing the thing out. We're done with it." Later, the other one would end up at a drugstore at 10 p.m. buying a new one, because we couldn't bear to let our son suffer. He had that pacifier forever—way too long, in fact. It wasn't until he was around nine years old that we finally got it away from him. Even then, it took an outside influence to make us change. His teeth were in bad shape, as you might expect, so we took him to the orthodontist. The orthodontist said, "I'm not going to put braces on you until you get rid of your pacifier." Our son came home, put the pacifier in a drawer, and never used it again.

Imagine our surprise. Turns out, he was fine without the pacifier, and would have been for years before that. We, his parents, were the ones with the problem.

The truth is that kids can tolerate hardship. It's really the parents who can't tolerate it—specifically, the hardship of watching their kids struggle and learn difficult but important lessons. Your fear as a parent of letting your kid struggle or suffer is ultimately really not about your kid at all. It's about your inability to deal with seeing your kid go through something that was hard for you as a child or not have something you deeply wanted when you were young.

NO ONE SAYS, "MY PARENTS TORTURED ME WITH PIANO"

Many people have stories from their childhoods about something their parents made them do: learn an instrument, play a sport, get an after-school job, attend tutoring. In a lot of instances, the enforced activity didn't last their whole childhood. At some point, the child complained enough to where the parent let them quit.

But when these people look back, few of them ever say, "I'm so mad at my parents for torturing me with piano lessons for six years." Instead, they say the opposite: "I wish my parents had made me keep going. It would be so cool to be able to sit down and play the piano today." Most people end up regretting what they didn't do, not what they did do.

At the same time, parents need to be very clear about their own motivations. Every parent brings personal motivations to how they raise their child, simply because they value certain things over others. These are sometimes cultural, sometimes religious, and sometimes based on the advantages and disadvantages of their own upbringing. While young children tend to accept and aren't conscious of feeling pressured by their parents, the truth can often be that the parent is creating a pressure-filled situation, not by virtue of the activity so much as the expectation around it. This is exactly the kind of pressure that gets escalated by the changes that happen in the teenage years.

Between growing up poor and having parents who lived in two different cities, I didn't get to participate in any league sports. This always disappointed me as a kid. So you can bet that as soon as my kids were old enough, I enrolled them in sports. By the age of four, each of them had started in AYSO soccer, and they continued well into their teens. For most of that time, they liked it. But at a certain point, my younger son began to push back. He said baseball was for me, not him. For that matter, so were his piano lessons and all the after-school tutors I signed him up for.

That pushback brought up an important issue for me to think through. It could have become an all-or-nothing issue—either he did all the activities I thought were good for him, or I let him quit them all because they were just "for me." (Years later, he told me that he felt I gave up on him because I let him quit. Sometimes you just can't win.)

It's important to remember that a kid will often resist the very thing they need in the moment. If a kid doesn't want to take piano or play a sport, you as the parent need to ask yourself, "What is the alternative?" In other words, what are they going to be doing in their new free time? Generally, it's not something better than the thing you've chosen for them.

Parents have to remember that their kid's responses to just about everything are transitory. How they feel about something right now is not how they will feel their whole life. Yet when parents hear, "You're torturing me," they react out of fear. They're either afraid of being bad parents, or they're afraid of conflict and dealing with a complaining kid.

When we look back at the shift in how children are raised that has occurred over just the past few generations, it's telling that even our word for it has changed. We used to call it "child-rearing." Today, though, we call it "parenting." This term puts all the focus on the parent—how they're performing, what they need and want from the experience. I probably don't need to tell you that this parent-focused approach doesn't have a great success record. If your goal as a parent is to turn out a high-functioning, independent human with a moral compass, who is competent and able to function in the world, you need to be making decisions based on something besides how raising a child makes you feel about you.

There's no doubt that parenting from fear is easier, at least in the short-term. It cuts down on interpersonal conflicts. It gets the room clean more quickly. It lets you not look like the bad guy. What it doesn't do is teach your kid anything.

Without struggling and undergoing hardship, your kid will never find out that they actually *can* get through hard times. Without experiencing the consequences for their choices, they won't learn how to take responsibility.

As a parent, it's not your calling to be your child's savior in times of crisis, especially the short-term variety. Neither is it your job to be their buddy or their "cool older friend." Decisions made with these goals will ultimately fail your kid. And chances are good that if you're reading this book, you've already realized that the decisions you've been making up to this point aren't working.

It's time for something new.

HOW CHILD-REARING WITH LOVE MANIFESTS IN BEHAVIOR

Child-rearing from love doesn't always look like it's making life easier for kids. Parents working from love have to fight their way through the short-term struggles to reach the long-term benefits.

As we talked about in the last chapter, a kid's problems are much harder for parents to deal with than they are for the kid. That's why parenting from love means frequently asking yourself who will be benefited by a given decision. You have to ask yourself, "Is this going to help my kid become a high-functioning, independent adult, or will it enable her?"

When a couple is about to have a baby, they're nowhere near ready to plan how the baby will grow up to be independent. They're too busy thinking about how they're going to care for, feed, and love that baby. If anyone were to ask those parents what their long-term goal is for that child, they'd probably say something like "having them grow up happy, healthy, and able to function independently." However, when the reality of independence begins to set in, those parents will almost definitely pull back. Some part of us wants to keep being needed. I still want my kids to need me, and they're twenty-three and twenty-five. It's not that I want them to move back in with me or anything. But I can remember that in the moment when they were about to leave for college, I didn't want to let them go.

Ten years ago, I was having lunch with a girlfriend whose daughter had gotten into both Stanford and Yale. She had to choose between opposite sides of the country.

I asked my friend, "Where do you want her to go?"

My friend said, "I would never tell her this, but I hope she picks Yale."

I said, "But that's so far. Aren't you afraid she won't come back?"

My friend smiled. "We don't get to keep them. I hate to break it to you, but there's a time for roots and a time for wings, and we're in the wings part."

I panicked. My kid could move to the other side of the country? I was *not* okay with that idea.

I realized then that I needed to pay closer attention to what I said to my kids. I didn't want them to feel they had to stay nearby to take care of me. I wouldn't let them become parentified children.

Kids are sensitive to this signal from their parents, and it's very easy for them to internalize the idea that their parents depend on them to be okay. That's how we end up with an allegedly gluten-intolerant kid gobbling down pizza while in session with me, but asking me not to tell his mom. He'd been made into a stranger in his own house by trying to please his parents.

If your kid senses you can't handle his struggles or emotions, he'll draw the conclusion that he can't handle them, either. This is incredibly damaging because one of the primary tasks in life is emotional regulation. Emotional regulation results from distress tolerance—in other words, building up your ability to get through hard times. Facing a simple problem teaches you not only how to solve the problem, but that you can survive it and come out okay on the other side. This is best learned incrementally. If you start small, you'll be adept at managing your emotions when the real challenges come.

This is why it's imperative that parents not rescue their children, especially not in the early years. If your seventh-grader tells you that the science fair is tomorrow and he forgot about his project, you must not stay up all night doing his project for him. No matter how much it kills you to think of him getting a bad grade, being scolded by the teacher, or standing there embarrassed with no project to show, it is crucial to let him experience this failure. He needs to find out that he can get through this hardship and draw conclusions about what he can do next time to avoid it. Let him undergo this bad experience, and it's a lot less likely that you'll be the one filling out his college applications for him in a few years.

I didn't appreciate my dad laying into me for giving away a box of candy bars, so I didn't treat my sons the same way. However, I also didn't find a way to teach them the same lessons I learned through that experience. Instead, they had to learn it later, in a more expensive way. Where I learned financial responsibility on a $30 box of candy bars, my son is learning it on a $30,000 Mercedes. (More about that later.)

As you go through life, you grow by learning what you're capable of. You are a completely different person today from the person you were ten years ago, mainly because of all the responsibilities you've taken on and the problems you've had to solve. The more hardship you overcome, the more confidence you have to take on new endeavors—moving to a new city, asking for a promotion, even having the kid that you're raising today. Facing hardship is how we grow. Because of this, parenting with love absolutely must involve teaching kids to tackle their own problems.

IF YOU DON'T RESCUE, WHAT DO YOU DO INSTEAD?

Not rescuing your child doesn't mean turning a cold

shoulder to their problems and struggles. Instead of leaping to fix problems and save your child from all hardship, you should seek to understand them and help them identify the underlying problems in their life.

When your kid comes to you with a problem, rather than trying to solve it for them, you can listen to how they feel. You can ask them questions about what they plan to do. You can prompt them to write out pros and cons. In all these ways, you can help them make the right decision without making the decision for them.

Good questions to ask include:

"What do you think you should do about it?"

"How do you think you can work through this?"

"Have your friends had to deal with this? What did they do?"

Another key role you can play is offering empathy and support. You can do wonders for your child just by saying, "Hey, that's a tough decision. I can see why you're struggling with that." Validating that the decision isn't easy lets them know you love them without taking the experience away from them.

For example, if your kid is putting off their college applications, you can ask what they're feeling that makes them put it off. You can follow up by asking, "Have you talked to a teacher or guidance counselor about this?" All of these are great alternatives to what many parents say instead: "You haven't turned in your applications yet? Let me call the school and figure it out."

HOW TO KNOW WHEN TO GET INVOLVED

As you can imagine, this approach is a lot easier with smaller problems. Lots of us can let our kids work through poor grades, bad friendships, credit card debt, or other natural consequences of bad choices. But what if those consequences are a lot more serious? Are you as a parent supposed to just ask questions and be empathetic in the face of suicide threats or dangerous behavior?

The reality is that certain situations need swift and decisive action. Anytime a kid threatens to kill himself, he needs to go to the hospital. Anyone can skip a meal, but if a kid is threatening to throw her food up, she needs to be taken to a doctor. If a kid is sneaking out to buy drugs or talking with older men in an Internet chatroom, they need intervention or therapy. When an issue is big enough that it prevents a kid from living their life or causes problems with school, work, or relationships, it needs to be managed by a professional.

As we discussed in the last chapter, parenting out of fear lends itself to the classic fear response of freezing. This, again, offers some short-term benefits. It's much easier for a parent to think, "This was just a one-time thing. All teenagers do this. She's going to be fine. She'll grow out of it." In other words, to convince yourself that something isn't a real problem, to escape the conflict that could arise from dealing with it.

However, talking yourself out of dealing with a problem is a lot easier than talking yourself out of worrying. If you find yourself spending a lot of time thinking about a problem your kid has, then guess what? It's a problem, at least for you, and you need to figure it out.

If you're unsure whether your kid needs professional help, there's an easy way to find the answer: ask a professional.

What this *doesn't* mean is trying to solve the problem yourself. If you're worried that your daughter has an eating disorder, don't do a bunch of online research and come up with your own treatment plan. That's just as harmful as ignoring the problem altogether.

When I talk to survivors of eating disorders and other self-harming behaviors, they often tell me, "I wish my parents had noticed and gotten me help earlier." Funny how that sounds so much like what people say about their parents letting them quit piano lessons: "I wish they'd made me stick with it." Kids might raise hell in the moment, but they'll be grateful later.

PARENTING FROM THE "ZONE"

In the 1930s, a psychologist named Lev Vygotsky developed a concept called the zone of proximal development. He developed it to better understand education, but I think it applies really well to parenting.

Vygotsky's "zone" concept says that kids learn by following an adult's example until they eventually become able to learn tasks on their own. To illustrate the concept, you can draw three concentric circles. In the center circle are tasks the child can do unaided at any given age, while the outer ring has the tasks a child can't do at all. The middle ring contains the tasks that the child can do with help.

This middle ring is the zone, and it is exactly where parents should be applying themselves while raising their child. If your child is an infant, you help them roll over until they can do it themselves. If your child is too young to ride a bike, you don't try to teach them—instead, you encourage them while they work on tying their shoes, or let them carry their own backpack.

Parenting from the zone means helping kids solve their own problems. It means having the love and patience to let them tie their shoes, even if it means you don't get out of the house on time. It means overcoming the tendency to do things for them that they can (and should) do on their own, so that they have the opportunity to function independently.

TEACHING BY EXAMPLE

Parenting from the zone also means leading by example. The way our kids learn from us is much more complicated than most of us ever realize. That's why, in order to effectively teach your kid, you need to first ask yourself some hard questions. As a parent, how do *you* problem-solve? How do *you* tolerate distress? How do *you* manage your life?

There's a saying that goes, "More is caught than taught." We don't realize that our kids are paying attention to us all the time. This is funny, considering how most adults are rarely aware of how they're acting, let alone being in control of it.

As a therapist, I will occasionally trace a line between a kid's drug use and their parent's drinking. I pursue this by asking questions about how the parent manages heavy drinking and being a parent. Most parents don't react positively when I say something like, "Your drinking has become a problem for your kid. Is it a problem for you? Are you willing to give it up?" However, it points out the essential principle that your behavior, as well as your words, needs to match the values you want to impart to your kids.

Kids' perceptivity will surprise you. Once, when I had a bad day, I kept talking about it. I told my kids; I called a girlfriend. A week went by. I brought it up again and one of my sons said, "Oh my God, you're still talking about it?" My other son said, "That's how she works through it." I hadn't even realized they were paying attention.

It's worth considering what your kids see from you on a daily basis. For example, what does your relationship with alcohol look like? Drinking alone? Driving under the influence? Missing work sometimes? This can apply to anything: exercise, work, friends, television, food, etc.

A lot of parents of drug users will tell me, "It doesn't make any sense that my kid is doing drugs. I've never done them in my life!" While it's true that your kid may not have learned the specific behavior from you, they probably have learned big-picture things from you about life that make health and sobriety more difficult for them.

You might be the hardest worker in the world, but if you come home every day complaining about your job, don't be surprised if your kid seems unmotivated to ever get one. After watching you suffer for so long, they're likely to think, "Work makes people miserable—I'm going to avoid it as long as I can."

The way you respond to them when they don't succeed right away also sets an example. If your kid tries to help you cook dinner, and you notice they're doing something wrong and say, "Oh, just let me do it," you've told them that they're not only incompetent, but also incapable of learning. Their brain is likely to apply that message to all kinds of things in the future—not just to cooking but to driving, or dating, or building a better career.

Again, it comes back to parenting in the zone. Instead of removing their struggle or ignoring it, you can offer advice and empathy. "The first time I did that, I had a hard time, too. You did a pretty good job for your first try. Let's try it again. What do you think went wrong last time?"

Doing a task alongside your child is often the best way to inspire them to do the same thing. I know a woman who was mesmerized by her mother's perfect three-movement shirt fold. As an adult, she now does it the exact same way. She didn't even notice when she learned it. She simply picked it up after a lifetime of seeing it done that way and trying to do it herself.

We all pick up methods from our parents. There's a story about a woman who cut the ends off her hams before putting them in the oven. One day, her husband asked, "Why do you always cut the ends off?"

She said, "I don't know. My mom always did that." She called up her mom and asked, "Why do you cut the ends of the ham off?"

Her mom answered, "My pan was too short."

We don't always know why we do what we do. It's just all we know. Whatever you do in front of your kids, that's what you're teaching them. That's why it's so important to be intentional about the example you're showing them. As a parent, that's pretty much your whole job.

PARENTS WHO WERE RAISED HARSHLY

Our generation has different problems than our kids. Many of us were raised to be high-functioning, but our parents were too harsh. We can cook and clean, but we struggle with feeling emotionally connected.

We didn't get enough praise or forgiveness. Unfortunately, parents today tend to lean too far in the opposite direction. That's how we've come to a place where it's normal for every kid in Little League to go home with a trophy.

I understand the fear of hurting your child through exposure to harshness and pain. But sometimes a harsh lesson is better than no lesson at all. If you're afraid to step in and teach your kid a lesson, ask yourself, "Is it more important for me to feel like I'm not my parents, or more important for my kid to learn how to function?"

If you don't teach your kid lessons, life will. And eventually, even you won't be able to soften the blow. You can only rescue your kid up to a certain point. Eventually, the authorities will get involved, or her boss will fire her, or his spouse will leave him, and there won't be anything you can do to make it better.

As parents, we think that we are helping our kids by protecting their feelings. But all we're really doing is saving ourselves from reliving the painful experiences of our own childhoods. We're saving ourselves while hurting our kids' chances to thrive in real life.

This isn't a black or white issue. You don't have to choose between teaching your child and being harsh, or not being harsh and not teaching them. Your words are inherently powerful, no matter what you say. Everyone's mom's voice rings in their head. Even when I look back at my situation with my dad and the candy bars, I realize he might not even have been as harsh as I remember. It could be that he was just so important to me when I was five, and my memory blew it up into something bigger.

The point is that you can teach a lesson through offering constructive criticism. You can even preface it with some softening words, like "This is going to be hard to hear..." That way, your child is more prepared to hear what you have to say, and knows that it's coming from a place of love.

CHAPTER THREE

SAVING YOURSELF

———

My parents divorced when I was four, and once I hit my teens, I became *that* kid. The one that every parent fears will result from divorce. I snuck out of the house. I ditched school. I hung out with older friends who weren't good for me. One time, I cut class to drive across the border to Mexico for the day, a classic misdeed for teens growing up in my hometown of San Diego.

I split my time between parents until I was fifteen. That year, my dad had had enough. After yet another rebellion, he laid down an ultimatum: "You're either grounded for a year, or you can go live with your mom."

For me, choosing option B was a no-brainer. As far as I was concerned, my mom had always been a pushover. On top of this, she was newly married and, with a teenager's unerring instinct, I saw how hard she was trying to save face with her new husband. In other words, I knew she was afraid of me and that I could get away with anything.

I took that power pretty far. Whenever I wanted to get out of school, I forged my mom's signature on a note to the school. The one time they called her to check, she actually covered for me. When I crashed my car, she helped me hide it from my stepdad. When the two of them left town for a week, they left me money for food and emergencies, which I promptly dipped into to get my nails done. Within a few days, the cash was all gone, but I wasn't worried. I simply used my forgery skills to write myself a check from her checkbook. What was she going to do? Call the cops on me, her daughter?

In all honesty, she should have done exactly that. There were no natural consequences for how I acted.

In a way, I guess I ultimately got my karmic punishment. Once I became a mother of teenagers, I was terrified they would act the same way I did. I worked overtime to keep them from learning any of the things I did as a kid. I shut down my sister more than once when she was on the verge of telling them what, to her, was a "funny" story about something I'd done as a teen. Yes, it was a good story, but I didn't want them thinking that kind of behavior was okay for them to engage in.

Some people might hear about my teenage shenanigans and insist I wasn't to blame. After all, I was just a kid. My mom should have asserted herself as the authority. Maybe I would have been better behaved if she hadn't been such a bad parent.

But being a parent myself and working with so many of them over the past several years, I see the other side of it. My mom wasn't a bad parent, pure and simple. She was a human being, blindsided by behavior she didn't understand and couldn't control, doing the best she could to maintain a relationship with her daughter who—let's be honest—was determined to get into trouble.

It's important for you to know that you're not a bad parent, either. How do I know? For one thing, bad parents don't read parenting books. Questioning your parenting is itself a sign of being a good parent.

There is always a reason behind the mistakes we make as parents. Maybe you were working two jobs to keep food on the table and simply couldn't be as attentive or present as you wanted to be. Maybe you were going through a hard time with your marriage or your health, and this kept you from being fully aware of what your kid was doing. Maybe, like my mom, you were just afraid that your kid would walk out the door and never come back if you didn't write their essay, pee in a cup for them, or cover their credit card debt.

Bottom line: your child's issues are not the direct result of your choices.

I remember observing a group therapy circle where one of the girls broke down into a temper tantrum during the session. The facilitator told her to stop and settle down; she responded by wailing, "I can't help it! I was adopted."

The facilitator said something I'll never forget: "Lots of kids are adopted, but they don't all act like you just did."

All parents make some mistakes. But not every child of parents who make mistakes becomes a drug addict, a criminal, or a burned-out loser living in the basement. You didn't cause this situation, nor did anyone else. You must let the blame go and look at how you can contribute to the solution instead of fixating on who's to blame for the problem in the first place. Forgive yourself and move forward.

YOU CAN'T (AND DON'T HAVE TO) DO IT ON YOUR OWN

I hear the same words from exhausted, worried parents over and over: "I can't do this on my own anymore."

They've been dealing with their kid's struggle for so long without any support that they're distraught. They haven't reached out to anyone, not even their social circle. They ransack the Internet for solutions, but their kid's problems just keep getting worse. As a result, the parent gets worse, too. They are trying to bring their family back to "normal" while experiencing off-the-charts stress levels. They don't realize that those stress levels would be a lot lower if they'd sought out help right away instead of trying for so long to do it on their own.

I know I've said it before, but I'll continue to say it: Why would you ever think you can deal with a dangerous or life-threatening behavioral issue on your own? If your kid started having seizures or developed diabetes, you wouldn't try to fix that on your own.

Few parents finally reach this breaking point without feeling guilty. They think, "Wow, I've been wrong for so long." They worry that they have ruined their kids' lives. But kids are incredibly resilient. Think back to your childhood—you survived, didn't you? You got through bad stuff, and you probably watched other people get through bad stuff, too. Your kids are going to be fine. Adolescence seems like a never-ending spiral downward, but eventually the teenager's brain develops, he realizes that life has consequences, and he starts making better decisions.

You can change, too. No matter what mistakes you've made—being emotionally enmeshed with your kid, trying to fix their problems on your own, or burying your head in the sand because it was all too overwhelming—you haven't disqualified yourself as a parent. Making mistakes is as normal a part of parenting as it is of being a teenager.

It's normal to take it all on yourself and feel a lot of shame around the things you've done or might have done. Every parent goes back and inventories their entire history with their child: "Things were never the same after I left her mother," a father may tell himself, or "This all started because I pushed him too hard in elementary school."

It's also normal to respond to that shame by justifying yourself: "Everything I did came from a place of love" or "I sacrificed so much to make sure this kid had a happy childhood." However, it's important to recognize that as a parent, you have a blind spot when it comes to the behaviors that actually contribute to your kid's problem. Their behavior could hinge on something you've never considered or even noticed. Even the things you think of as solutions could themselves just be more problems. Generally speaking, this isn't something you can figure out on your own. (That's kind of how blind spots work.) You need an outside perspective to get started. That's true for every parent, even me.

YOU CAN'T MAKE YOUR KID CHANGE

I know that you would do anything at all for your kid. If there was something you could give up, or some crazy task you could complete, just to make your kid get out of bed, stop throwing up, or find some motivation, you would definitely do it. But this is the very thing you have to work on in yourself: knowing that you *can't* make your kid change. No matter what you do or say, no matter how much you research their problem or how many techniques you try.

The only thing you can do is learn to let go and focus on really loving your kid. Again, I know that all the things you're trying to do come from a place of love. But real love means recognizing what's out of your control—their choices—and working on what *is* in your control. The only thing you can control is your response to their choices. You can enable their behavior out of fear, or you can respond out of love.

I understand that making this shift is difficult. If you've been focused for the past two years or more on "fixing" your child, or if you feel swamped with guilt and shame over the mistakes you've made, it will take time and effort to shift your perspective from fear to love. When you've grown accustomed to parenting out of fear, it may even feel impossible to change.

> Would it surprise you to know that your kid proba-
> bly feels the same way you do? The teens I work with
> often express doubt that their parents can ever stop
> responding to them out of fear and a desire to control.

If you stay in a place of self-loathing, nothing will improve. But by recognizing your capacity to change, you can overcome your shame, anger, and fear and learn how to parent out of love.

GETTING STARTED—AWARENESS IS KEY

When I had teenagers, the idea of shutting off their cell phones scared the hell out of me. If I took away their phones, they could go out, and I wouldn't know where they were!

See how it was more about me than about them? But after a while, parents have trouble seeing the distinction.

When interacting with your kid, put understanding and awareness first. Say your son comes home drunk, or you catch your daughter cutting herself. You will feel fear. You'll want to get angry, yell, demand an explanation, make him or her confess everything to you. Ultimately, though, what outcome do you want? Not for you, but for your child?

You're a good parent. What you want is for your kid to be okay. If that's what you want, the answer is clear as day. To make sure your kid is okay, you need to get him help. If you can come from a place of calm, you can find the right solution—the one that comes from love instead of fear.

This is not a one-time act. Each time a problem arises, you have to return to this place of calm, decide what your desired outcome is for your child in the long term (not for you in that moment), and think logically through how you can get from here to there, step by step.

I have a teen client who had a pattern of self-harming, partly stemming from depression. She signed a contract with her mom to abide by some house rules. The cardinal rule was that if she smoked a cigarette or vaped, she would lose her cell phone for a month. One day her mom called me to say she'd caught her daughter vaping in her bedroom.

"Okay," I said. "Take her phone."

Two weeks in, the mother called me again. "You know," she said, "my daughter says that because she doesn't have her phone and can't talk to her friends, she's feeling very isolated. She's afraid that without her phone, she's going to get depressed again."

I said, "Don't you dare give that phone back. You do that, and you've lost all ability to parent."

The daughter knew her depression was a trigger for her mom. By threatening that it might come back, she could easily get her mom to do what she wanted. (Later, she even admitted to me, "Yeah, I was totally manipulating her.") Even her mom knew this is at some level. But in that moment of intense fear that her daughter would become depressed and self-harm, all she really wanted from me was permission to give in.

When parents question, "Should I do this?" they generally know the answer. If you find yourself unsure of what to do, stop and ask if you're really that confused, or if you're simply rationalizing. It's so much easier to give in to fear by continuing to do what you've been doing, e.g., enabling your child's behavior, than it is to begin the Herculean task of changing tactics.

But remember that by continuing to do what you've been doing, you're helping your child continue to do what they've been doing. Change only happens as the result of experiencing the natural consequences of our choices.

INVENTORY WHAT YOU'RE TEACHING BY EXAMPLE

To understand your kid's behavior better, you need to be more aware of how you're living your life. For instance, are you constantly stressed and over-scheduled? Do you seek reward or escape from shopping, overeating, drinking, spending all day on Facebook, etc.? Do you overreact when you're upset or say or do things you regret?

Your teenager's behavior may look nothing like yours, but it very likely has similar roots. What kinds of situations or stresses drive you to behaviors that aren't the best? Your example is teaching your child how to respond to those life situations. How do you respond to the slow checker at the grocery store? How do you react when the refrigerator breaks for the third time? In the face of stress, do you complain, self-medicate, shut down, or problem-solve?

Changing from fear to love requires awareness of what you're teaching your kids to expect out of life and what life will expect from them. If you feel frustrated because your kids seem to live in a bubble of laziness, entitlement, and irresponsibility, consider how they might have gotten there. Could it be that your fears drove you to build that bubble around them as a means of protection? Does love look more like keeping them in that bubble, or allowing natural consequences to take their course?

TYPICAL STUMBLING BLOCKS

Parents have a habit of making their jobs much harder. They do this through putting up a series of stumbling blocks for themselves that affect their ability to understand what their child is going through and/or assess the best way to handle it.

STUMBLING BLOCK #1: ASKING "WHY?"

Everybody wants to know what made their kids start engaging in harmful or dangerous behavior.

"Why did she start cutting herself?"

"What made him think it's okay to skip school?"

"How did my kid get hold of drugs in the first place?"

Changing from fear to love means resisting the question "Why?" Blame is useless when it comes to solving problems. Like fear, it's primarily self-centered—it does nothing to help someone change.

Parents who fixate on "why" are usually looking for some evidence that it's not their fault. Either that, or they are torturing themselves by searching for evidence that it *is* their fault. In both scenarios, that parent is adopting the position of victim.

The victim role is a handy one, because it absolves you of responsibility. But without taking responsibility, you can't change. Everyone involved in a problem needs to look at their own part in it and not take more or less of the responsibility than is truly theirs.

Now, you might be somewhat justified in pointing the finger at, say, your ex-wife or husband, or at one of your child's friends. However, it's unlikely that you didn't also contribute to the problem in some way, even if it was just by "loving your kid to death."

It's an uncomfortable truth to deal with. But the upside is that taking responsibility gives you some agency in the situation. By changing the part you play in your child's life for the better, you can help change the entire situation.

I have a client with a tragic story. When she was sixteen, she sneaked out to a club and was victimized by someone there. Her parents wanted to blame her, given that she knew better than to go to a club where she wasn't legally allowed to be. The kid's regular therapist wanted to blame the parents, saying they were so permissive, she had no reservations about sneaking out to go there. I listened to this back and forth for a while, before I finally said, "Guys, stop. None of this matters. What happened, happened— we can't take it back. At this point, the question is how are you contributing to the problem, or to the solution? That's the only thing you can change, going forward."

Your kid's problem may not be a recent phenomenon. It may have roots that go way back. Something bad may have happened when the kid was really young, but the trauma didn't present itself until they reached their teens.

I've brought this up to parents only to have them claim, "Well, such-and-such did happen when they were three. But they weren't traumatized—they got through it just fine." What these parents don't realize is that, as we discussed in Chapter Two, their child's brain didn't fully process the event at the time. The trauma hung around in the child's subconscious until he or she was a teen, at which point the brain developed the capacity for mental and emotional response to the event. Until the brain gets to that point, you can't really know how a trauma has affected a child. And the sad truth is that some things can't be fixed—at least not in the sense you want as a parent.

If your child is struggling with deep-seated issues that come from traumatic events, you need to understand that you can't fix her. She isn't "broken." She had a terrible experience that is now part of her makeup, and she needs help in moving forward from it. Seeking a way to make it as though the bad thing never happened will only make her issues worse.

STUMBLING BLOCK #2: DEALING WITH BACKLASH

In my experience, stressed and anxious parents do not want to hear that there isn't a "fix" or cure for their child's behavior. Dealing with their kid's issues one day at a time, making slow but steady progress through holding boundaries, is hard work. Especially when the backlash hits.

As soon as you start setting boundaries, you can expect your kid's behavior to escalate. When they realize that you've changed the rules on them, whether it's consequences for their misbehavior or simply making them do things for themselves, they will fight back.

You think you're prepared for this, but actually dealing with it will be hard for you when it happens. Depending on the day or the situation, you'll have trouble holding your ground. No matter how prepared you are, you'll feel awful hearing "I hate you," or "If you don't do this, I'm going to hurt myself again." You'll start thinking how much easier it would be to give back the phone, call the school, pay the bill, etc. You'll worry that if you change what you're doing, your kid will fall a lot harder.

It's hard to keep your head out of a place of fear. But you must be strong. The goal is to raise independently func- tioning humans. The more your kid depends on you, the less self-esteem and confidence they'll have.

STUMBLING BLOCK #3: NOT DEALING WITH YOUR OWN BAGGAGE

Almost none of the parents who walk into my office are aware of the baggage they're bringing with them. They come ready to unload all their kid's baggage onto me—their history, their issues, their patterns. But when I start to ask parents about their own lives, they shut down.

People don't want to look at the baggage they carry, even when it's pointed out that they are projecting their baggage onto their kids. As hard as it is for a parent to see their kid struggling, it's often a whole lot easier than looking at themselves. I've noticed that for some of them, fixating on the kid's issues is a habitual way to avoid opening the Pandora's box of their own life.

When it comes to things like deep-seated emotional issues, if you don't have the ability to recognize yours, you're never going to be able to help your kid get through theirs. You need to figure yourself out—and quickly—so you can effectively help your kid.

STUMBLING BLOCK #4: NONLINEAR PROGRESS

Parents need to know from the outset that for a kid engaged in problem behavior, progress is never linear. He used to isolate himself, but now he's suddenly mouthing off to you all the time. She was starting to eat more regularly, but now her weight is down again.

Your first reaction will be, "Oh my God, we're right back where we started." When that happens, take heart. It's just a dip in the road. When a swimmer gets a shoulder injury, they stop swimming. However, they still know how to swim. Your kid still has their new coping skills. They just didn't remember to use them on that particular occasion. Backsliding is a normal part of forward progress.

IT'S NOT LINEAR

A SETBACK IS A

dip

NOT STARTING OVER ...

THEY ARE AFTER ALL OPERATING WITH A TEENAGE BRAIN.

Resist the urge to fall into a place of fear. Don't react to the backslide by trying to retake control or saying things that communicate hopelessness or blame. Your best move is to stay in a loving place and keep focusing on changing the ways you contribute to problems in the family.

If your kid notices their own backsliding and starts blaming you for it, don't argue with them. Say, "Look, I made mistakes as a parent, and I'm still learning too. I'm sorry. But now it's your problem. What are you doing about it? As long as you're blaming me, you're not getting better."

WHY CHILD-REARING WITH LOVE IS HARDER THAN PARENTING FROM FEAR

Child-rearing with love sounds a lot nicer than parenting from fear, doesn't it? But the reality is that it is much, much harder to do. While no parent actively thinks, "I prefer fear to love," many have trouble letting fear go. When we fear that our kid will end up dead, that fear is hard to overcome, even when we know it won't help.

Parents are naturally inclined to believe that if they can just take control, nothing bad will ever happen to their kid. But that is not a sustainable model for parenting. Short-term measures lead to short-term results, at best. The long-term solutions work precisely because they take place over a long period of time—long enough for the kid to learn a new way of living. And there's no way around it: applying those long-term solutions takes a lot of hard work from the parent, particularly emotional work.

One of my clients was a teenaged girl whose behavioral issues were negatively impacting her younger siblings. Knowing this, I advised her mom to sign the girl up for a wilderness program.

The mom was in tears at the idea of letting her daughter out of her sight for so long. She said, "I don't know if I can do this."

I completely empathized with how she felt. But here's what I said:

"When you're deciding where to have your daughter's bat mitzvah, or picking out a birthday present, parenting is easy. This, on the other hand, is one of the tough parenting moments. You have to make this decision based on what's best for your child, not for you."

Party planning is fun, but that isn't real parenting. Real parenting requires emotional control, especially when your kid is out of control. It requires hard decisions that are based on a desired long-term outcome rather than the short-term rewards.

I go to the gym almost every day. I can't say I enjoy it; there are a hundred things I'd rather do with that time. But it's a choice I make to get the long-term outcome I want.

Parenting from love requires you to examine your own agenda. When you think about your hopes for your child—going to college, being successful, picking the right partner—whose benefit are you mainly thinking about? When you say you want to be a better parent to your children than you had, are you prioritizing your child's well-being or your own?

ALL CHANGE IS HARD

By the time parents come to me, they've already gone through some heavy changes. The years of trying to manage their child's problem on their own have taken a toll. They don't look at their kid or at parenting the same way they used to.

Some parents will say, "I'm done with this kid—I've tried everything, and I give up." Others say, "I can't ever detach from this kid; I have to do so much for them." Both perspectives indicate a history of enabling. And while I hate saying it, it's true that very bad things usually have to happen in order for parents to realize they're being enablers.

At the same time, if you and your teen have been locked in a cycle of bad behavior and enabling for several months or even years, the prospect of change can be genuinely scary. Change requires doing things that are unfamiliar, including, in some instances, acting directly against your instincts.

This why I always recommend parents get a second opinion about their family's problems. When you're in that window of wanting change and fearing it at the same time, you're so emotionally involved that you probably can't see the forest for the trees. Talking to more than one professional will help you see the bigger picture and develop more self-awareness around what really needs to change, both in your own life and in the way your family operates as a whole.

CHAPTER FOUR

UNDERSTANDING YOUR KID

———

A number of years ago, I was moving out of my house into a new one. My older sister and my friend Katie came by to help me. Moving is always an organization game, and at one point, the three of us faced a bottleneck of boxes, furniture, and other things in the hallway. My sister surveyed the situation and said, "Let's get this table out of the way." She looked right past me toward Katie and said to her, "Come on, you grab the other end."

Katie looked at me and then back at my sister. She gestured at me. "What, are her arms broken?"

Katie couldn't understand why my sister and I both burst out laughing. It was just another example of a dynamic between us that goes way, way back. When our parents divorced, as the older of two latch-key kids, my sister naturally fell into the caretaker role. My mom left for work before the school bus came, so it was my sister who made sure I had shoes on and got out the door on time. Throughout our early lives, she was the responsible one who looked after me, the incompetent one. As a result, even when I was in my mid-thirties, with a husband, a family, and a doctorate, she still instinctively took on the burden, leaving me with no responsibilities at all.

I don't do much to disabuse her of this instinct. When our families get together at her home for holidays or other events, I immediately revert to my teen role. While she's going a mile a minute in the kitchen, getting everything ready, I'm usually kicked back on the sofa, relaxing. When I do offer to help out, she turns me down. Neither of us usually thinks to question it.

It's an almost universal truth that when people return to their families of origin, they fall into the roles they inhabited growing up. It's not intentional—it's just how family systems work. This situation is so common that a whole psychological concept has been built around it. It's called Family Systems Theory, and it goes a long way toward explaining why it's so hard for you and your teen to change your dynamic, even when you both truly want to.

FAMILY SYSTEMS THEORY

Developed during the 1950s, Family Systems Theory is about viewing the family system as a whole and determining how it affects each person within the family. According to this theory, you can't understand an individual in isolation from others; instead, the family functions as a system, with each member having a role and rules. As I like to explain it, families are like cogs in a clock, with all the pieces turning in response to each other. If one piece is removed, the other ones work together to compensate for the lack of that piece.

FAMILY roles

HERO

SCAPEGOAT

LOST CHILD

MASCOT

Often, this is necessary, and it's not always bad. When my parents separated, my sister began over-functioning to compensate for what she felt as a lack of caretaking from my parents, and it was a really good thing she did. I hate to think where I'd be today if she hadn't been looking out for me.

I know a family in which one of two daughters has Down's Syndrome, and the other is a perfectly behaved over-achiever. The latter feels she has to be this way. For one thing, her sister's limitations make her keenly aware of the advantages her abilities offer her. For another, she knows she's likely to be her parents' only opportunity to see their child succeed in conventional terms: go to college, be successful, and have children of her own.

In other words, Family Systems Theory is not always about decreased functioning. Sometimes the system demands better functioning to keep running; one goes up when another goes down. But it makes it easy to see how individual family members tend to assume or adopt certain roles that they grow to own over time. In response to my sister assuming the caretaker role, I compensated by doing less.

One of the most seminal early studies in Family Systems Theory came from observations of schizophrenic children being treated in a hospital. After working with therapists and physicians for a number of months, these children showed remarkable improvement and were sent home to their families. Once they were at home, however, their symptoms returned. Soon, the hospital staff began bringing not only the schizophrenic child in for therapy, but also the entire family. The result was sustained improvement in children's health and ability to function.

The researchers studying this phenomenon realized that the patient's symptoms didn't occur within a vacuum. No matter how much improvement a patient experienced in treatment, returning to the old family environment immediately provoked them to decompensate. In order to maintain their improvement, the entire family system needed to improve.

Whenever someone in the family—be it the parent or the kid—shifts the balance of the family system by making different choices, it causes a subtle but powerful shift in the way everyone else operates. You've already experienced this with your teenager. As they have functioned less, you've been functioning more to compensate.

No parent compensates in this way with the intention of setting up a perpetual system for their family. Instead, it starts as a one-time rescue. Your son's grades start to drop because he's not doing his homework. Afraid that his GPA will slip, you complete an important end-of-year assignment for him and tuck it into his backpack. You might not ever talk about it with him, but the system begins to shift. He does less, you do more, all in order to maintain the status quo.

Parents who do things like this never feel quite right about them. So why do you do it? The reason usually comes down to feeling like a bad parent if you don't. You don't want your kid to fall behind academically; you don't want him to have to attend summer school; you don't want him to fail a class, not get into a good college, and never have the chance for a good career as a result.

But take a closer look. Whom are you really doing this for? Is doing your son's homework benefitting him? Or is it benefitting you?

 This is a question I have to ask parents all the time, and it's not their favorite one to answer. It's not easy for anyone to say, "You know what? I'm doing this for me. I'm doing it to make me feel like a better parent or to make me feel needed and indispensable." This does not make them bad parents, and in asking this question, I'm not intending to cast blame. It is, however, about recognizing that sometimes the things you do to *feel* like a good parent will make your kid less likely to be independent. It takes a parent with a good sense of self to admit that they're preventing their kid from getting better.

WHEN THE SYSTEM BEGINS TO SHIFT

Ultimately, this is a book about parenting, not about curing your kid. Remember what we discussed in the last chapter—you *cannot* change your kid. Their changes are up to them. What you can change is the part you play in the system that influences their choices.

Just like Newton's law, for every action, there is an equal and opposite reaction. Be aware that when one part of the system shifts, either in a good or bad direction, it's inevitable that the rest of the system will shift as well.

Any time you make a change to the system, you can see in real time how the system reacts. Oftentimes, that reaction looks like a revolt. So as you begin to make changes in your parenting, consider the possible reactions to your actions. If you don't take your kid's homework or lunch to school, what will happen?

Let's go back to the homework example. Midway through the day, you get a text from your son. "Where's my assignment?" You'll answer him, "Right on the table where you left it." He'll be surprised and dismayed—this wasn't what he expected—and as a result, he'll be angry at you. He'll begin to catastrophize about the consequences, pushing all the right buttons he knows will trigger your anxieties. "You have to bring it, or I'm going to be in trouble. This teacher already hates me. I'm going to fail this class."

You'll start worrying that your son will flunk out, drop out, or not get into college, and this will make you want to jump in the car right now and take him his assignment. These are all normal parts of the adjustment to change.

When a kid goes into therapy, they need to know that while they are making changes in treatment, their parents are making changes, too. If they come back from therapy to an unchanged home, they will go right back to their old ways. *You* need to work to maintain the changes they've made. If you've learned to set boundaries, parent with love, and detach from their problems, your kid's recovery is much more likely to stick.

ADOLESCENCE IS TRAUMA

Erik Erikson was a pioneer in adolescent development. The main takeaway of his research boils down to a simple fact: adolescence is traumatic. Even without drawing any external traumatic events into it, the changes that take place during adolescence in a young person's body are dramatic, overwhelming, and sometimes even violent.

Culturally, we acknowledge many of the changes that happen to teenagers at a hormonal level. But very little is discussed about what is happening within their brains during this time.

Adolescence brings a new phase of development to the brain, but it doesn't happen all at once. Teenagers begin thinking in new ways and want to try them out, much the way an infant wants to experiment with pulling itself up or walking across the room. However, a teenager trying out their new brainpower looks a lot like arguing, asking uncomfortable questions, and making controversial statements, sometimes on purpose, sometimes not. They suddenly have the ability to question the things their parents have been telling them all their lives. They also realize they could fall in love with a person of another race or culture, discover a sexual orientation other than heterosexuality, or change their religion. Wires keep connecting in their brains, and they want to experiment with what happens when they begin discussing those connections aloud.

Unfortunately, parents tend to freak out in these moments. Rather than recognize conversations with their teenagers as opportunities to help their minds develop and let them try out new ways of thinking in a safe environment, many parents react in fear.

For example, when you hear your kid say, "I'm thinking about getting a tattoo," you snap back, "Over my dead body! You'll never get a good job with a tattoo." When you hear your kid ask you, "What if I married someone of a different race?" your mind veers toward all the systemic cultural issues they and your future grandchildren are likely to face. (Or maybe just to how uncomfortable it would be to introduce your elderly uncle to a spouse of a different race at the family reunion.)

As long as your kid is not making actual choices resulting in long-term or permanent change, there's every reason in the world to let your kids think about whatever strikes them. While sometimes their statements and questions are about genuine values they're beginning to have, their comments are often hypothetical—your kid is simply inviting you into her thought process. She also might be testing the waters to see how a given choice would affect your love for her. She could also be trying to differentiate herself from you by trying on something that, to her, represents the opposite of who you are.

A kid's goal is to become their own person, and they do that by being different from what they know. They want to explore what it's like to be perceived in certain ways as well as how people respond to different personalities. Teens have not yet learned how to differentiate in a healthy, moderate way, so they tend to go to an extreme in their early attempts. However, the majority of kids return gradually to the ways that they grew up with, since those ways are familiar to them.

While some kids are more oriented toward talking these

brain developments through, others are more prone to actively trying on new identities as a way of experimenting. This often takes the form of how they dress and the persona they adopt. When I was a teenager, I wore plaid shorts and put safety pins in my earring holes—I was very drawn to the Brian Setzer "Stray Cat Strut" look. That's why, when kids come into my office with hair that's blue, green, or pink, I say, "Oh my God, that's gorgeous." Their parents are probably freaking out, thinking that it means the beginning of a steep decline in their child's future. But I know it's just an experiment—and a temporary one at that. Things like clothes, hair dye, and piercings are easy ways to try on a different identity, as they try to figure out what about it appeals to them.

As a young child, your kid only believed what you told them. As a teen, he or she is gaining the ability to reason and think differently. When your teen argues, resists your authority, and fights back against the boundaries you've set, he or she is practicing this ability. And that's actually a good thing!

But despite how normal it is, parents still take it personally. It's common to assume that your kid's actions are a direct and personal response to you. You will find yourself shocked by behavior that is totally normal, or even relatively good. As a parent, it's natural to believe that if you program your young children with the right values (i.e., the values you want them to have), they won't rebel as teenagers. Nothing could be further from the truth.

A teenager's brain is wired to rebel, though not in a malicious sense. They're simply learning to think for themselves for the first time. It's the same phenomenon as when your three-year-old pushes you away from trying to help her get dressed, saying, "I can do it myself!" When she proudly emerges from her room with everything on backward and upside down, you probably don't take that as a personal reflection on your worth as a parent. Instead, you laugh internally, congratulate her on how hard she tried, and show her how to fix what she got wrong.

It's hard, but not impossible, to take the same approach with your teenager's experiments in identity. When your kid proposes getting a tattoo, says she's joining the Peace Corps after high school, or announces he is not sure the male gender is right for him, you can look at it as an opportunity to help him or her expand their ability to think rationally and critically. Instead of jumping to the worst possible outcome of this line of thinking, you can ask your kid what got him thinking about this and help him explore what about the topic is appealing to him.

Ultimately, these actions from your teenager come back to the central purpose in adolescence: they are pushing the boundaries they grew up with. That is their job as a teenager. Your job as a parent is to hold the ones that matter.

SO WHICH BOUNDARIES SHOULD I HOLD?

As the parent of a kid undergoing the seismic shift that occurs during adolescence, it can be very hard to know which boundaries you should hold and which ones you should let go.

A good place to start is with examining your own motivations around certain standards in your house. There is no time like adolescence for parents to discover how much of their self-worth is tied to their kids. The boundaries that you're imposing strictly because of your values (like the mom who insisted her kid eat "gluten-free") are a lot less important than boundaries on illegal activity or objectively harmful behavior.

For example, a lot of parents these days are hearing their kids push back against rules against smoking marijuana. "Oh my God, mom. It's not a big deal. Everyone smokes weed." Of course, that is not an objectively true fact. But the kid probably believes it, because in his small world, it's true. Regardless of where you live or what your politics are, the fact is that it's still illegal for teenagers to smoke marijuana. When your kid pushes against this boundary, you don't have to rationalize it to yourself, saying, "This is just what teenagers do. I'm going to look the other way." But you also don't have to look twenty years down the road and think that your kid's interest in smoking weed today means he's going to end up selling drugs on the street while living in your basement. Instead, you can hold the boundary with a simple statement of fact like this one:

"Actually, not everybody smokes weed. It's not legal for someone your age to smoke it, and it's not okay in our house. That's not something I'm going to support, and here's what the consequences will be if I find you doing it again."

Although many of the boundaries you set may be necessary and effective deterrents to illegal activity or objectively harmful behavior, others are likely to be based on your individual values. These are very easy to rationalize—you probably have them for reasons that are perfectly clear and valid. But imposing them on your kid is a sign of fear-based parenting and therefore often needs to be adjusted to let your kid experience and learn from natural consequences.

For example, if your daughter struggles with anxiety, attention problems, and insomnia, but drinks five cups of coffee a day, it's probably time to set a boundary. However, it should be based on objective, observable facts, not on your feelings about what's healthy and what's not. You can say to her, "If you want to drink coffee, that's fine, as long as it doesn't lead to you staying up all night. If it does, you're not going to drink it anymore."

I set a similar type of boundary with my son. He wanted to go to bed a lot later than I thought was advisable, especially considering how it affected his attitude and behavior the next day. But rather than badger him about it, I let him make the decision himself. I simply set the boundary ahead of time: "You can stay up. Just remember that generally, when you don't get enough sleep, you're grumpy the next day and cause problems at home. If that happens, you're going to have a curfew." That approach created self-awareness and personal responsibility, and it helped him manage his own life better.

You'll be surprised to see how often your teen knows you're right. He might even acknowledge it—"Oh yeah, that's true. That does happen." The point is to make the boundary about your kid and his or her well-being, not about you and your preferences. You can't babysit a teenager's caffeine consumption or choice of bedtime forever. At some point, kids need to take the responsibility and consequences on themselves. But you can be a part of enforcing those consequences and making sure they take responsibility for their decisions.

Of course, there are situations that fall into a grey area, such as eating disorders, self-harm, and suicide threats. While these behaviors aren't illegal, they are very dangerous, and it's understandable that they would provoke a fear-based response in the parent. There is a middle ground to holding this boundary. You can't sleep on your kid's floor throughout her life to make sure she doesn't self-harm, monitor every calorie she puts in her mouth, or drop everything to intervene each time she threatens to kill herself. But you can let her know that when these things take place, the consequence is that she's going to end up in a linoleum-floored room with really bad food and a pesky doctor like me asking her a lot of questions.

BRAIN DEVELOPMENT IN TEENS

The field of brain research has advanced a lot in the last ten years. We now know that it takes a long time for the "Jell-O" to set, as it were. Not until a person's early twenties do all the adolescent changes in their brain take a solid, established form. When that moment finally happens, there's an "ah-ha" moment for the young adult. They look back and say, "Oh my God, I'm so lucky I'm not dead." Up until that moment, they thought they were invincible. Thinking for themselves required a certain amount of foolish conviction in their own logic.

You can tell a kid, "Don't put yourself in this situation,

because this bad thing might happen," but odds are they won't believe it. They generally don't have the same level of fear as adults. Their brains haven't yet fully developed that response to future possible outcomes.

That's why, for example, drug prevention programs don't work. Kids who go through the D.A.R.E. program in elementary school will earnestly pledge never to use drugs, but once adolescence sets in, all that education does nothing to stop them from trying drugs at a party or a friend's house. Their understanding has changed from the conceptual to the experiential. They try the drugs and think, "I'm not dead, and I didn't feel terrible. That was actually fun. Those people who said drugs were bad were lying to me." Their brains haven't developed enough to consider the possible long-term effects of drug use against their immediate experience of it.

Your teen's brain doesn't process danger the same way that yours does as an adult. They aren't going to be scared of the things that scare you, no matter how well you explain it to them.

THE COGNITIVE TRIAD

A therapist can intervene in a person's thinking at three levels: thoughts, feelings, or behaviors. All these levels all interact with each other. For instance, take the thought women always have: "I'm fat." That thought starts a chain reaction that translates into emotions (frustration, depression, apathy) and then into behaviors (bad nutrition, disordered eating, significant health problems). However, if a woman starts instead with a thought like "I have a strong, healthy body," she is more likely to feel positive and proactive, and follow up those feelings by eating healthy food and having good exercise habits.

Psychologists call this interaction amid thoughts, feelings, and behaviors the Cognitive Triad. What's really interesting about it is that all the elements lead back to each other. In other words, if you can shift any one of the three, the others will shift as well.

As a parent, this is invaluable information. It shows how creating a shift in the overall family system can force a shift in a kid's behavior, which then influences a shift in their thoughts and feelings. If your daughter does poorly on a test, and you express your fear that she'll never get into a good college (whether that means laying into her, or simply letting it show on your face), it will affect her self-confidence. Those feelings will influence her thoughts and behaviors going forward.

This also works in reverse. If you don't think smoking marijuana is a big deal, but you tell your kid "That's not allowed" when you find out he is smoking, he will know whether he's really in trouble or not. He'll see from your response whether there will be consequences for doing it again.

A NOTE ABOUT BEING THE "COOL" PARENT

Trust me, you don't want to be the "cool" parent. That strategy always backfires. Your kids will use it against you, saying, "You can't tell me not to do this when you did it, too."

It's true that kids with strict parents look at their friends' "cool" parents and think, "I wish my parents were like that. They're so relaxed and fun to be around." But the actual kids of those parents don't think that way. They never think, "Wow, Mom is really cool. I think I'll listen to her more." What actually happens is that they lose respect. More importantly, they lose a sense of security. While kids might push you away, they need you to be a parent, both structurally and emotionally.

This cognitive triad also applies to your own thoughts, feelings, and emotions. When a parent says to me, "If I don't bring my kid their homework, they're never going to college," I try to shift their perception of the situation to something constructive. Thinking "They're never going to get to college" engenders negative emotions and behavior. In contrast, "If I don't bring my kid their homework, they'll survive, and they're going to learn an important lesson" engenders positive feelings and behavior.

I want to reemphasize that you can't directly change how

your kids think, feel, or behave. What you can change is how you respond to them, which has the potential to influence them to change on their own.

REMEMBER, ADOLESCENCE IS TEMPORARY

The good news is that while adolescence is an incredibly challenging time for kids and parents, it is temporary. In fact, it doesn't last for very long, though for the adolescent brain, it definitely feels more like a marathon than a sprint. And for a parent, it can feel equally excruciating.

Leading up to this marathon, parents really need to take care of themselves. It's downright foolish to try and weather your kid's adolescence with your emotional resources depleted. You'll be completely drained before you know it.

As a parent, you need to take care of your own mental health. Go to bed at a decent time. Reach out to your support system. Read a good book, get a massage, take the afternoon off to sit and stare at the ocean. Do anything you can to work on yourself, because you're going to spend six to ten years in a period of upheaval, change, and conflict in the family system.

Parents frequently tell me that they can't make time to take care of themselves in the way I suggest. What they often really mean is that they feel guilty for making time. They look at the struggles happening in their family system and think, "Why can't I manage this?" They think it means something is wrong with them.

Depending on where you live, there may not be widespread approval for parents taking care of themselves. Despite the growing cultural emphasis on the importance of self-care, parents still worry that others in their community will see them taking time for themselves and think, "Oh, that parent is so selfish. They went and got a massage."

It's not selfish to take care of yourself or indulge in time alone. But it can be difficult. When I was a parent, I struggled to do this. It was rare for me to leave my child overnight. I did it maybe once in the first few years. Any time away from my kid made me feel guilty.

I don't think that's an ingrained instinct. I've had friends who would go away for the weekend or even longer, leaving the baby with grandma, and felt fine about it. I don't know why they could do it without guilt while I couldn't. I suspect it all comes down to the different personalities and experiences that make us who we are. It's probably no accident that I became a therapist—one of a big tribe of people who all want to care for others and fix everything.

There's a famous quote that goes something like this: "I'll

take care of me for you, if you take care of you for me." It sounds simplistic, but it's something you absolutely have to do as the parent of a teen. In order to fix the family system, you have to start by fixing yourself.

In a lot of ways, it's easier to focus on your kid's behavior because it seems so black and white. The good and bad choices that your teenager makes are so obvious, it can make changing your own thoughts, feelings, and behavior seem ridiculous. I've had parents respond to me by saying, "What do I need to work on myself for? I'm not the one with the problem." And I've countered such comments with, "If it's not your problem, why are you trying to fix it?"

Fixing your kid is a pointless task, one that will drain your energy and leave you feeling more frustrated and inadequate than when you started. Your best hope is to become the impetus for change by changing how you parent.

CHAPTER FIVE

MAKING CHANGES

———

Not long ago, I was watching my twenty-two-year-old son roll up an extension cord. He was winding the cord around his arm, with his hand near his shoulder. He was basically tying himself up in front of me. Watching him, I couldn't help but think of all the things I could do while he was tied up, like take his fancy Mercedes for a spin, or snap an embarrassing photo of him and post it all over social media. What can I say? Sometimes moms have the instinct to torture our kids. (Just a little.)

Of course, we also have the instinct to rescue them. Even while thinking of all the fun I could have at my son's expense, I was about to take the cord from him and do it myself. But I remembered the "parenting from the zone" concept we talked about in Chapter Two, and stopped myself. Instead of taking it from him,

I explained it to him, giving only the information he needed to do it on his own.

"You know, you're tying your arm up in there," I said.

He looked at me. "What are you talking about?"

"Try to pull your hand out," I said. "See? Pull your hand away from your shoulder or your arm is going to get tied up in there."

If I'd taken the cord from him and wound it myself, I would have been communicating that he was incompetent, and it would have damaged his confidence. But through my teaching him, he learned how to do it on his own.

MEETING YOUR KID WHERE THEY ARE

As a new parent, you might have been given a development chart that told you when you should expect your new baby to roll over, eat solid food, and begin trying to babble their first words. But there aren't hard and fast rules about when teens are developmentally ready to learn different things. Each teen's overall progress and specific benchmarks are very specific to them. That's why it's best to teach as experiences present themselves to your kids, even when those opportunities end up happening in a kid's early twenties, like I did with my son and the extension cord situation. It would never have occurred to me in parenting my son as a teen to pull him aside and say, "Okay, let me show you how to wrap up an extension cord." It wasn't on a list of milestones—the opportunity just presented itself that day.

Problems are opportunities for teaching, and they come up at every age. As a parent, you will always have more experience to draw upon than your child does. Effective teaching is all in how you approach it.

TIPS FOR HELPING YOUR KID CREATE THEIR OWN SOLUTIONS

Part of parenting is teaching kids how to connect the dots between their experiences and the choices they've made. If they feel depressed, why might that be? Did something happen that day? Did they make bad choices that left them hungry or sleep-deprived? Have they been fixating on negative thoughts? Leave the answers up to them, but prompt them to make those connections.

Even as adults, we have moments where we feel depressed, anxious, or dissatisfied with our lives, and we have to make changes. We all have to learn to make those changes for ourselves without relying on another person to make us feel better or give us solutions.

As a therapist, I ask questions to gauge where kids are with their emotional skills. If a kid says, "I'm starting to feel depressed again," I ask, "What coping skills are you going to use?" and "What can you do to feel better?" I steer clear of saying, "Why don't you do this?" or "Next time you're in this situation, just say this to yourself."

GUIDING YOUR KID TOWARD SELF-CARE

At the end of the last chapter, we talked about the importance of self-care. You need to replenish your emotional resources to get through the traumatic period of adolescence. Your teen, who is going through the same exhausting, demanding process you are, needs the same type of replenishment. The kid who is depressed and lying in bed all day isn't just doing it to piss you off. They're doing it because their tank is at a low level.

The best types of treatment programs don't focus exclusively on correcting bad behavior. They look at fueling good behavior through positive experiences and energizing activities. And as we talked about in the last chapter, intervening at the behavior level affects thoughts and feelings, motivating better choices in turn. When you feel better, you do better.

For example, the treatment programs I recommend usually combine mindfulness practices with activities like yoga and outdoor adventures. I've seen unbelievable changes in formerly depressed kids after just one day of surf therapy. At the very start, the instructor asks the kids, "All right, before we get in the water, what are we leaving on the beach?" They all get a minute to think about it. Then they go into the water. The instructor gives them a push, so it's easy for them to catch their first wave. Their amazement at discovering this new ability helps disrupt their pattern of depression. Along with the many documented benefits of nature, the endorphin rush brought by exercise gets their good neurotransmitters going.

Bottom line: good self-care measures like mindfulness, exercise, and outdoor activities give kids a moment of relief—a moment in which they don't feel terrible. If adolescents can put together as many moments like this as possible, then they have the best chance of healing, surviving, and getting through this tough period in their lives.

DRAWING YOUR KID'S FOCUS TO THE RIGHT PLACES

Being in an argument makes people tend to focus on what's happening in that moment. You get caught up in the detail—tones of voice, choice of words, the immediate outcome you want—and forget to look at the bigger picture of what the argument is about.

As a parent of a teen, your job is to lead your kid out of those distracting details to focus on the content of the argument. What are they arguing with you about? What is so important to them, and why? Join them in considering how they got to this point. Treat the cause, not the symptoms.

These tips can help. But remember, you can't fix your kid. You might have been trying to get your kid to practice yoga forever, or to engage with you calmly instead of arguing, but they dug in their heels anyway.

When it comes to sustainable change, there's really no substitute for therapy. It's simply easier for kids to make changes in their behavior and thinking when they're in a new environment—particularly when they're surrounded by other kids doing the same thing. However, you can work on yourself so that when your kid returns to the family system, it's able to support the changes they've made.

CHANGING THE WAY YOU THINK

After everything you've gone through with your teenager, it's understandable that you might have a hard time seeing your kid or your situation clearly anymore. At a certain point, you might just see your teenager as a failure—someone who is beyond your help or anyone else's.

It's terrible to suspect this about your own child, but it's easy to get there when you're emotionally exhausted.

I promise you, you don't have a bad kid. Their bad choices are the result of pressures, struggles, and challenging experiences they are going through. It's important to reframe your thinking from thinking, "There's something wrong with my kid" to "My kid needs help."

Along with changing the way you think about your kid as a person, you need to examine how you think about them in relationship to you. We make parenting decisions based on our own expectations and desires, without even realizing it.

One of my clients was thirteen years old and Jewish, which meant she was getting ready for her bat mitzvah. Her mom happened to mention that she wasn't going to throw her daughter the traditional lavish party. No matter how well she planned it, the mother said, something would inevitably go wrong, and then she'd just feel angry and resentful at having spent all that money and it not turning out well. Instead, she told me, they were planning a family trip to New York City. They'd stay at a nice hotel, go see a Broadway show, enjoy a fancy dinner.

Later, though, the mother complained to me that her daughter was digging in her heels, refusing to go on the trip. "I can't believe this," the mother said. "I put all this work into planning this great trip, and now she says she isn't going."

I said, "If you want to go on this trip, you should go. But you need to acknowledge who the trip is really for."

"What are you talking about?" the woman said. "I'm doing this for her!"

"Are you sure you're not doing it for yourself?" I answered. "You're doing it for yourself. It just happens to be scheduled around her birthday. That's fine, but don't put your expectations on her. You know that if you take her on this trip when she doesn't want to go, she's just going to end up sabotaging it."

I've heard this same refrain from parents about any number of things. Piano lessons are a big one. I have seen parents buy pianos only to end up with a big new piece of furniture collecting dust. Nobody uses it, but the parents still keep the piano. Maybe it's because they always wanted to learn piano as a child. Or maybe it's because it feels good to brag to their friends that their kid plays an instrument. If the kid isn't interested in the piano, though, it's clear who this decision is really for.

School offers up another great example. Many parents have told me resentfully, "I can't believe my kid is failing out when I paid for them to go to this amazing private school." But no kid has ever asked to go to an amazing private school.

Sometimes, parents can get so caught up in their own agendas that they don't even see where those agendas have come from or whom they're benefitting. We sometimes plan things that will benefit our kids but we do it because *we* want them to have the experience, not because they want the experience. In many situations, parents are healing their own wounds by putting them on their kids. But that approach never works out as planned. Not only does the kid push back against it, but the parents take it personally when their kids don't follow the path they've set up for them.

Parents often believe they are doing things for their kids when in reality, they're putting their own values onto their kids and trying to give the kid what they—as the parents—want. That thing might even objectively be a privilege. The problem is that it's not the one the kid asked for. Parents in this situation can end up resenting their kids for being ungrateful. And their kids can end up resenting being pushed to enjoy something they didn't ask for and acting out in response.

CHANGING THE WAY YOU LIVE

Kids are very sensitive to conflicts at home as well as con-
tradictions in their parents' behavior. When a kid feels like
they need to walk on eggshells around their home or that
their parent is focusing on them as a means of distraction
from their personal issues, it creates a ripe environment
for them to engage in destructive or dangerous behavior.

I work with a number of teens whose parents will bring
them to therapy, enroll them in treatment programs, and
do anything else that they think might help their kid. But
if I recommend these parents attend a parenting class,
sign up for personal therapy, or make other necessary life
changes, they dig in their heels. They tell me they're not
the one with the problem. It's true, they aren't in the same
danger as their kids. But in many cases, a kid's problems
can be a side issue that would magically go away if the
parent would be proactive about changing their own life.

One mom I know was trapped in a terrible marriage for
ten years. Every time she and her husband tried to get
divorced, their conflicts only got worse. It was easier for
her to back off and switch her focus from the terrible
marriage to her child's mounting behavioral issues. The
problem, however, was that the child's issues directly
resulted from the conflict in the home. By not working
on the real problem, she was unwittingly exacerbating
the situation.

One kid we worked with struggled with depression and suicidal thoughts. As we worked together, he told me that his parents fought viciously all the time. Following that session, I told the parents that they needed to stop fighting in front of their son. If they wanted to fight, they should either do it somewhere else or make sure he wasn't in the house when they did.

Only a week later, at our very next session, the kid told me it had happened again. The previous night, his parents had gotten into yet another big fight. "My dad had to sleep on the couch," he said. "I feel bad for him." It was horrible to see what a weight this boy was carrying, as a result of his parents' decisions.

I brought in the parents to ask about the argument. "I know you love your son," I said. "We discussed how much the fighting is hurting him, and you agreed not to do it in front of him. Therefore, I have the feeling you can't control it." They agreed. "You guys need to separate while we're doing this work," I continued. "You can't live together."

In that moment, they agreed they couldn't control the fighting and that it was making their son's issues worse. But as the conversation continued, it became clear that they still had a vested interest in continuing their toxic dynamic. The mom was angry at the dad for any number of things, big and small, and wanted to go on punishing him. She wasn't interested in changing her life at that time. (I don't think she ever spoke to me again after that meeting.) The dad, however, did take the steps I recommended. He got an apartment of his own. After their separation, the kid's depression dramatically improved.

Another more difficult situation involved a mom whose son's behavior was way beyond her control. He was a teenaged "Dennis the Menace" kind of kid, who was acting out in all kinds of harmful ways. Her daughter, meanwhile, had recently started refusing to go to school.

The mom told me that a big part of her children's problems was their dad. He was barely involved, she said, and saw the kids only once a year. When he did see them, he was mean, so the kids didn't like being around him.

Oddly enough, on the kids' very first day of treatment, I received three calls from the dad. He asked me detailed questions about the program and what his children would be doing. He also paid the deductible over the phone. Later, I learned from the kids that their dad called them every day and came out to California from Atlanta once a month to visit.

The mom had painted a very negative picture of the dad that simply wasn't accurate. In order to get the full picture of the situation, I arranged to meet with the entire family one weekend. During the session, the mom began to nod off in her chair. I looked at the other family members who didn't seem to flinch, saying, "Does anybody else see this?" A few questions revealed that she was sleepy from the pain medication she took for an old sports injury. It had been an ongoing issue. Her daughter walked in on her one morning when she was passed out, couldn't revive her, and had to call 911. (It became apparent why the daughter was refusing to go to school. She was likely afraid something would happen to her mom, and she wouldn't be there to stop it.)

When anyone pressed the mom on the subject of painkiller use, she would snap at them, "I don't have a problem."

Obviously, the son's problematic behavior came from a much bigger root than simply his issues, or even the father's role in his life. By coming to the mom from a loving place and helping her see the need in her family for her to acknowledge the problem, I managed to get her to agree to go to treatment.

It was a big shift, but it happened quickly. Within days of that session, we had arranged for the kids to move to Chicago to live with their dad. Our staff actually picked them up and took them to the airport. The original plan was for them to come back after their mom completed treatment, but they're doing so well there, they ended up staying. Soon, they were doing well in school and making friends. The daughter took singing lessons, while the son became a state-ranked gymnast. And once mom had dealt with her issues, she was able to provide the structure and support her kids needed to thrive in life.

> Sometimes, when a kid goes into treatment, it's the parents that need the most support. This is the only time fear-based parenting is useful—when it inspires a momentum shift.

I understand that sometimes, it's hard to acknowledge the real issues in your kid's life. But as hard as it is to control their behavior (or try to), you might find it's even harder to acknowledge the ways that your own behavior or lifestyle contributes to it. After all, acknowledging this makes it real. (To you, anyway. To everyone else in your family, it's the elephant in the room that nobody talks about.)

For the good of your kid, it's time to get your head out of the sand. Don't run away from the situation. Press into it. Even if it's hard, you *can* make changes in your life and household. You need to. Your kid needs you to.

HOW YOU CAN SWITCH TO LOVE

Switching from fear to love requires big changes in how

you parent. One of the first things is to begin learning how to manage your fear. Even with the best intentions, your efforts at love-based child-rearing can't be effective when fear is getting in the way.

LET YOUR KID BE WHO HE/SHE IS

Even the best parents don't slow down enough to really listen to what their kid wants or needs. Even when they do listen, if they don't agree with what the kid is saying, their instinct is to try to shut it down. This gets in the way of one your kid's greatest needs from you: acceptance and approval of who they are.

You might not like the way your teenager dresses, eats, talks, or spends their time. You might wish they would join a club, play a sport, or get more exercise. Those behaviors aren't objectively right or wrong. They're just your preferences, and your kid knows it.

Most of the time, a parent's preference has to do with what they perceive as the easier, less painful way. As parents, we try to guide our kids down the path of least resistance, not because of a certain ideology, but because we want to protect them from struggle. We want them to have an easier life, and even the most open-minded parents fear their kid making choices that they believe could make their life harder, like not going to college, or having non-traditional sexuality.

In contrast, a real problem is missing 100 days of school in a year, not being able to hold down a job, having legal issues, or being stuck in unhealthy relationships. Those are real problems worth focusing on.

You need to be more objective when it comes to identifying problems versus preferences in your kid's life. If your kid's personality, values, or goals for their life don't fit your plan, bite your tongue and deal with it. Remember, it's their life, not yours. You may think your daughter's future happiness and success depends on her becoming a doctor, but who is going to be putting in the sixty-hour workweeks in that career? She is, not you. Becoming a doctor had better be what she wants if she's going to do it.

From the moment I started thinking about higher education and career, I wanted a degree in psychology. I was fascinated by the class titles in the course catalog. But when I mentioned this to my stepdad, he said, "What are you going to do with a degree in psychology? You can't do anything with that. You should become a teacher. That way, you'll have good benefits, and you'll have summers off to spend with your kids." (He also recommended that I enroll at UCLA, where I would meet a man who would treat me the way to which I'm accustomed.)

I didn't end up at UCLA, but I did take a stab at the liberal arts. I remember sitting in an education class, learning how to teach math, thinking, "What am I doing? This isn't fun. I'm not enjoying this." It wasn't long before I dropped out of school altogether. Many years later, I went back to school for—you guessed it—a psychology degree. Turns out, you can do a lot with such a degree, particularly when it's a field you really love.

If your kid wants to be an artist, a musician, or an activist, don't shut her down. Remember, it's more likely than ever that most people will have more than one career. It's equally likely that their career path will be distantly related, at best, to the degree they get in college. What really matters in terms of their college degree is that they get one, not which one they get.

Focus on what really matters in your kid's life. Are they healthy and maturing? Are they applying themselves to what they want? Are they functioning independently? When you try to put your kid in a box, you do much more harm than good. But when you accept them for who they are, they will learn to value their own life, skills, and potential.

FIX YOURSELF FIRST

So many parents fixate on their kid's success (or their

perception of it) as a distraction from the ways they themselves are not successful. You can't tell your kid he can't smoke marijuana if you're self-medicating with alcohol. The mom with the painkiller addiction was pushing her kids to be responsible and go to school, while she wasn't being at all responsible in her own life. Neither are the myriad parents who insist their kids go to treatment but won't set foot in a therapist's office for their own issues.

Instead of trying to weed all the issues out of your kid's life, ask yourself, "What am I doing with my life? Is it just focused on my kid? Am I practicing what I preach?"

One boy was enrolled in my treatment program for a marijuana-related problem. At the outset, he seemed to enter the program willingly. But after a week, when his parents visited, the kid pulled his dad aside and said, "You're going to take me home today. If you don't, I'm going to tell mom about the text messages to some woman I saw on your phone."

I know about this because the dad shared it with me immediately after it happened. I said to him, "You know that if he's successful in holding this over you now, he has you hostage forever. If you give in, at some point, you'll end up buying him a Ferrari to stop him from telling his mother."

He said, "I know, I know."

The dad agreed that we'd address the situation during our afternoon group session with his wife and son. However, I fully expected the dad to not hold the line. In fact, I immediately began strategizing about how to manage the kid's exit when the dad pulled him out of the program.

To my surprise, though, the dad dropped the bomb at lunch. He told his wife about the text messages. At the time, I thought it was amazing he did. In hindsight, he might have been finished with his marriage and looking for a way to end it.

It makes intuitive sense that when parents do the right thing in their own lives, they are better able to draw boundaries.

START MAKING THE HARD PARENTING DECISIONS WITH CONFIDENCE

You might be afraid to take away the phone or Internet access, stop bringing your kid his lunch and homework, or say "no" in any given situation. What if your kid rebels even more, or suffers even worse, as a result of your holding boundaries?

Parents voice these concerns to me all the time. My response is usually something like, "I know. God forbid your kid has to live without the Internet. Whatever would he do?"

You *can* make the hard choices. You can handle the backlash. It comes down to fighting for what you know is right. Even making that decision is easier than you're probably making it. A helpful rule of thumb is that if you asked yourself whether it's a good idea to just give in, it's not.

You'll be surprised by what a powerful shift happens when you start making the hard decisions. Your fear disappears, and your self-esteem improves. This makes sense. After all, as we've discussed, our self-esteem comes from the choices we make. While it feels bad in the moment to take your kid's phone away, it feels a lot worse in the long-term to allow them to skip school, indulge their drug habit, or look the other way when they're engaging in dangerous behavior on the Internet.

Education is key in developing the confidence to make those decisions. Consulting your support system—whether it's a therapist or someone else who can guide you—is key to separating the behaviors you don't like from the behaviors that are truly problematic. This is crucial in creating boundaries that you can abide by.

> One good thing about having a treatment team is that you can redirect the kid's anger to their therapist or program. When you say, "Your phone has to be plugged into the outlet in our room one hour before you go to bed," you can include, "This is what your treatment team recommended." That way, your kids can't get mad at you.

Remember, kids are resilient. They are great at finding ways to lash out, but they are also great at adapting when they realize those methods aren't working.

I work with some parents who drop their kids off at treatment with the attitude of "My kid is broken. Fix him/her." I've been asked to do everything from make sure the kid has a healthy lunch to take away a kid's vape pen. I've even had parents say, "While he's here, can you take him to the dentist to get his teeth cleaned? I haven't been able to get him to go."

It goes back to my friend Katie's response to my sister overlooking me, while we were moving. "What, are her arms broken?" Your kid is not broken. His body and mind still work the way they are supposed to. As the authority in his life, you are the one who is supposed to hold the boundary. Remember, you have all the real leverage in the relationship. You pay for the phone, the groceries, the car, the Internet. Your kid depends on you for everything. Use that to your advantage in getting the ideal result: a high-functioning, independent adult.

CHANGE YOUR THINKING ABOUT MENTAL HEALTH

Health isn't black or white. It occurs on a spectrum. Even among people who are considered healthy, there are some who are in great shape and some who just don't have any chronic issues (yet). That's why the healthiest people always look for ways to stay well and even get better.

Mental health is no different. At least, it shouldn't be.

Our society has a perception of how people with mental illness look. We might call someone with over fifty cats "crazy," but that's not a mental health issue. "Has too many cats" is not a diagnosis.

The fact is that nearly everybody has mental illness at one level or another. When people have mental health problems, their first move is to put up defenses to hide the issue, even from themselves. They rationalize their behaviors until they feel it's acceptable, meanwhile failing to address the underlying problems.

Just the other day, a teen client in my office asked, "What exactly am I working on? I don't even know. Why am I here right now? I've made a lot of improvement." It was almost funny, given that just a week before, she'd tried to jump out of a moving car. Still, she thought that if she wasn't lying in bed or actively trying to kill herself, she didn't need help.

The stigma around mental health needs to be broken. The perception that people either have mental health issues or they don't is false. Anybody who has a brain has mental health issues. As we go through life, we manage better sometimes than others. Health is not linear. Even if you've never dealt with a particular issue, you may still get it someday. Certain circumstances or events may make you more vulnerable to mental illness, or it may present itself suddenly.

I have a torn meniscus in my left knee, but I walk, run, and keep up with life as well as anybody else. Nobody would know about my injury if I didn't tell them, but I don't have to hide it out of shame. I just take care of it, do what I can to heal it, and get it checked regularly. Why wouldn't you take the same measures for your mental health? After all, the brain is a muscle. The same principle applies to any other muscle: if you don't use it, you'll lose it.

HANDLING BEHAVIORS YOU DON'T LIKE

As parents, we tend to freak out about the wrong things. We can see one problematic behavior that looks familiar to us—smoking pot, sneaking out, underage drinking— and not worry about it too much. After all, we did it, and we turned out all right. But when we see our teenager cutting herself or spending all day in online chat rooms, it freaks us out.

Freaking out is never the answer. The answer is to get help. Sleeping on your daughter's floor to prevent her from cutting herself or using your son's password to log into his computer to see what he's been doing online is not a sustainable solution. A parent can't live like that. Moreover, you can't cure something you didn't cause. Even if your behavior contributed to or influenced your kid's behavior, at the end of the day, their actions are their choice. Your kid needs to do the work. Your job is to teach them how to do this work through your example, the boundaries you set, and the consequences you enforce.

As we discussed in Chapter One, when you're confronted with a behavior you don't like, your first urge will be fight, flight, or freeze. You'll want to get angry and yell at your kid, hide from the issue, or get trapped in a spiral of worrying while doing nothing.

Instead, your first recourse should be to get your kid help as you also begin working on changing your behavior. I recommend that parents look into Al-Anon. While this program is designed for the loved ones of alcoholics, it's all about understanding codependency and enabling within relationships. These principles are extremely helpful in recreating the family system we discussed in Chapter Four.

Once you've decided on reasonable boundaries to address your kid's behavior, you need an arsenal of responses to the inevitable backlash. One of my personal favorites is,

"What you're doing isn't working for me." It's not meant to be an argument. There is nothing for the other person to say in response. (We'll talk more about good responses to backlash a little later in the chapter.)

As for enforcing consequences, it's important to remember that they happen on a continuum, commensurate with your child's age. Parents tend to think, "If I don't make sure my kid goes to college, I'm either going to support him for his entire life, or he'll be homeless on the street." They use this extreme thinking as an excuse for giving in to the kid's behavior.

Here's the thing: if your kid fails a class in high school, the worst that's going to happen is that he has to go to summer school. If he fails a full year, he's going to have to repeat it. If he doesn't get into college right away, he's going to get an entry-level job. None of these things involve you supporting him all his life or him being homeless on the street.

The same principle applies to many behaviors, including criminal offenses. You may not realize that a kid's legal records are sealed until they turn eighteen. In other words, now is the time for them to learn what it means to stay on the right side of the law, while there are some protecting factors in place. When they're adults, the consequences are more severe, and their record becomes public.

> I realize that there are certain situations, especially regarding a teenager's health and safety, where the consequences are immediate. If a dire consequence occurs, you can at least know you did everything in your power to prevent it.

Recently, a client in my residential therapy program needed a higher level of care, but her dad was reluctant to pay for it. On the other hand, he had just written a check to a woman to pay for damages to her car that his daughter had caused. This father was fine with paying to protect his daughter from legal consequences, but he did not want to pay for her issues to be addressed. He was just putting a Band-Aid on the situation without healing the wound. By doing this, he was setting himself and his daughter up for a situation that would only get worse and involve more severe consequences, financial and otherwise.

Believe me, I know how hard it is as a parent to just sit back and watch while your kid suffers the consequences of his or her bad decisions. Even when we know our main job is to teach our children to do something for themselves, whenever we have the opportunity to do this, we still feel and often succumb to the urge to do everything for them.

This might help explain why parents react to their kids becoming independent by instinctively trying to hold them back. That's where the Family Systems Theory from Chapter Four really comes into play. It compels you to take an honest look at your family and realize that even positive changes are still major shifts in your family balance.

THE EXTINCTION BURST

Think back to the child in the checkout line who is used to getting candy every time they whine for it. The day their mom finally says "no" and sticks to it, the whine will turn into a scream the whole supermarket can hear. If the mom tries to stop the screaming, the kid will begin to thrash around and may even run away from her. In that moment, she can do one of two things. She can give in out of embarrassment or fear, and teach the kid that screaming is rewarding. Or she can push through the humiliating situation, get the kid home, and teach them a new meaning behind the word "no."

You need to anticipate that whenever you set a boundary, hold a limit, or change the rules, your child's behavior will almost definitely get worse before it gets better. This is known as the extinction burst. It might look like an emotional outburst (especially in a public setting), a volley of hurtful words and threats, or bullying you while you're trying to work or relax.

Here is how to survive the extinction burst:

BE PREPARED TO TOLERATE IT

If you're not taking care of yourself and don't have much energy, it's a lot easier to give in and reward your child's bullying behavior. They'll see that it works, and, next time, they'll just try harder. You need to ride it out. If you hold the line, eventually they will stop.

KEEP YOUR RESPONSES LOVING AND SHORT

Some good responses include:

"I know this is hard for you, but we're not going to go back to the way it was before."

"I should have never let it get to this point. But this is what we're doing from now on."

"I'm sorry you feel that way."

And of course, my favorite:

"That doesn't work for me anymore."

Understand that change is difficult for your kids and be willing to empathize even while you're holding firm. Here's a tip that may help: If your kid is acting out more, it's a sign that you're on the right track.

Parents tend to panic if a kid becomes more vocal about their bad behavior, i.e., threatening out loud to cut herself instead of just doing it and you finding out later. Hearing her say things like this, it's easy to think, "Oh my God, it's worse than before." Actually, the vocalization is a sign of progress. The kid is speaking her mind instead of internalizing everything.

Keep connecting to the place of love and hold firm. If you can get through this phase, change is right around the corner.

TYPICAL CHALLENGES IN SHIFTING FROM FEAR TO LOVE

Parents can act like just like the kid screaming for candy in the checkout aisle. We know how to manipulate them almost as well as they do us. And if we see that nagging, yelling, or harping on our kid produces a result, even just one time, we'll go back to that approach again and again.

Child-rearing out of love isn't about controlling your kids. It's about understanding when what you're doing isn't working for your family and changing the dynamic of how you all interact.

However, there is a learning curve to parenting this way. Here are some of the typical challenges you're likely to face:

SETTING CLEAR EXPECTATIONS AND CONSEQUENCES

For many of the years I spent raising my kids, I'd come home from work and immediately go into maintenance mode. I'd walk in the door, toss an empty Coke can left on the counter into the recycling bin, move a pair of shoes from the living room, throw away a wrapper from the coffee table.

I could have made my sons come downstairs to throw their own trash away. But I just did it myself. It was such a little thing, I told myself, it shouldn't bother me so much. But it did bother me, and I built up a ton of resentment with every Coke can I tossed in the recycling bin. That resentment came out in full force whenever my sons made a minor infraction. If they did something I had specifically told them not to do, I would blow up at them for it. To them, it looked completely unfair...and it was. I was actually punishing them for all the behavior I'd resented for so long rather than the immediate behavior.

Setting clear expectations is foundational to shifting your family dynamic. Make sure you're willing and able to follow through on the threats of consequences you make—that you don't simply issue idle warnings in anger. Threatening to send your daughter to boarding school if she doesn't shape up won't help you achieve the desired result if you can't afford to send her. Not allowing your son to get his driver's license is a misguided threat of a different type—driving is a life skill that you actually want him to learn.

If you explain your expectations and the consequences for not meeting them, there's no need for a fight, and you won't end up over- or under-punishing your kids. If you give in constantly to their behavior, only to shout "You're grounded for a month" when you reach a breaking point, your kid will be confused and learn nothing from the situation. Your kids need to know what to expect so that they can learn how to make their own choices.

> Not laying out your expectations clearly also sets up a situation for not holding boundaries. I work with a kid whose phone got taken away as a consequence for leaving his backpack on the floor. He'd been told not to do it, but he'd never been told what the consequence of not doing it would be. Admittedly, it was a consequence that was not well aligned with the behavior. In the kid's eyes, it was completely unfair, unrelated, and unexpected. The day after it happened, though, he showed up to his session with his phone. "How do you have your phone back?" I asked. "I thought you said yesterday that it was getting taken away for a month."
>
> He shrugged. "With my parents, that's just kind of how it goes." His parents realized that the consequence was overreaching, so they'd given in to his demand they return his phone. As a result, the kid experienced no consequences at all.

CHOOSING THE RIGHT MOMENT TO INTERVENE

Consequences are important, but they don't always change behavior. We see this in people's health all the time. If it just took a little pain or suffering to set us straight, nobody would be overweight, or drink too much, or smoke. Even though being overweight causes joint pain, drinking gives us hangovers, and smoking kills people, these long-term consequences generally don't motivate people to change.

Consequences only work when they're swift, severe, and happen in the moment. In other words, if you have a bad day, you shouldn't punish your kid for something she did two weeks ago. (Although as parents, we often do.) The consequences must happen in the moment, and they must be related to the offense.

The best way to create change is to teach the kids to connect the dots. If a kid stops using drugs, and they feel better with their head clear, they will be motivated to continue. When someone is trying to lose weight and they hear, "Hey, looks like you've lost a few pounds," they feel good, and they are motivated to keep trying.

CREATING A SUSTAINABLE BEHAVIOR PLAN

When you're addressing a behavior that doesn't work for you, consider that it *is working* for your kid. In other words, they're using that behavior to get something they feel they need.

When you communicate that your kid's behavior isn't working for you anymore, take the opportunity to create a plan that involves their well-being. Along with explaining the consequences for the behavior, set up new privileges to be earned by not engaging in the behavior for a certain amount of time. Then stick to the plan you communicated. If a kid's needs are being met, they will likely comply with the plan.

Wondering what to say to a child in order to start changing their behavior? Instead of the emotional outburst that never changes anything, it can help to follow the "When You/I Feel/If You/I Will" script. Here's an example:

When you come home late for your curfew

I feel concerned for your safety.

If you come home late again,

I will move your curfew to an earlier time.

For example, one plan might be that a kid must be home by 11 p.m., and for every fifteen minutes they're late, their curfew becomes thirty minutes earlier. That way, your kid can be having a good time at a party or watching a movie with friends, but she knows that fifteen minutes that night will cost her a half-hour the next. She might still make that trade—maybe it was a really good movie, or maybe she was having a great conversation that she didn't want to leave. Making that choice is up to her. You don't need to yell at her (even though you might be inclined to). Instead, you can simply just say, "Well, you know you have to be in thirty minutes earlier tomorrow."

Kids like a little give and take. Odd as it may seem, if you don't try to fully control them, they're more likely to follow the rules you set. We recently worked with a girl who always took her meals to her bedroom, which was not working for her mom. They negotiated having dinner at the table but snacks in her room on the condition that she always clean up. Another client had Internet privileges taken away because he was spending all day online, engaging with strangers. After his behavior improved, his parents allowed him to have Internet access again, but they told him that they would be monitoring his time and activity and have access to his passwords.

Compromises like these give your kid freedom with responsibility. Offer your kid a little part in the decision-making process, and you might be surprised how well it goes.

Remember, controlling your kid is not a sustainable way of life for you or for them. At some point, you have to let them out of your sight. You can't constantly supervise them or prevent them from ever doing anything that might make them suffer.

BEING CONSISTENT

A huge source of parent-child conflict is having a set of rules that changes all the time. Kids need consistency in order to learn how to make choices. They need to know what you expect by when.

Obviously, you can't do this with every responsibility or chore. Taking out the trash is something that needs to be done on-demand, for example. Start with something that can be consistent. Perhaps it's that your son's bed needs to be made before he leaves the house in the morning, or perhaps the grass has to be mowed before he can go out for the weekend. Another effective approach is creating a list of things that need to be done by Friday at 5:00 p.m. (or whenever you choose), but letting your kid decide when to get those things done. This way, within certain parameters, kids have some semblance of control over their own lives.

Keep the big picture in mind as you enforce boundaries and be flexible when it makes sense. If your teen had to be up early for some student body meeting, it's okay to give him a pass for not making his bed that day. It's important to keep perspective. Just because a kid didn't respect a boundary one time under special circumstances, it doesn't mean they'll go back to where they started.

Of course, for the more important boundaries, like maintaining sobriety, going to meetings, or not engaging in self-harm, there should usually be less flexibility around consequences. However, it is important to consider the circumstances around the relapse. For instance, if your kid has been using secretly for three weeks and you catch them, that's a different situation from their using once and immediately calling their sponsor.

CAVING IS BAD; COMPROMISE IS GOOD

Giving in to your kid's behavior enables their poor behavior and prolongs the toxic pattern in your family. Compromise is a different animal. It involves give and take, the acknowledgment that both parties have preferences, and there's a way to make sure everyone's needs are met. Remember, your kid's brain is in a state of rapid maturing. This puts them in a great place to learn how to think through both sides of the situation and advocate for their own needs while acknowledging yours.

We worked with one kid who wanted to do her homework at the kitchen table. However, the table was a kind of mecca for the home—her siblings' kids were there watching TV, her mom was there making dinner or talking on the phone, and of course, people were always either eating or about to. When the parents insisted she clear off the table for dinner, she ignored them. When they demanded that she do her homework in her room, conflict erupted. Finally, the three of them came to an agreement: the kid couldn't complain about the noise around her or ask everyone to be quiet. In addition, she had to have everything cleaned up to her mom's satisfaction by supper time. If she couldn't do those two things, she would have to do homework in her room. That kind of bartering and compromise is normal.

Compromise has to be based on objective needs, not on a person's individual preferences. If you're a health-conscious mom who is bothered by how much coffee or soda your teenage daughter drinks, step back and evaluate. Is it affecting her life? Is it interfering with her ability to function? If it is, you can set up a compromise: whenever you notice she isn't sleeping, or that her anxiety is increasing, she has to stop drinking coffee. But if she's able to function normally, don't make her caffeine intake a problem just because you don't like it.

Your child's willingness to compromise with you is a good gauge for where they are in their recovery. If they can't adhere to reasonable arrangements—if they aren't going to therapy, are consistently late for school, or keep going back to the same behavior that produces the same results—it's time to bring in outside help.

Don't let compromise take you back to enabling behavior. I knew a kid who would take off on his skateboard whenever things got bad at home. In response, his mom began hiding his shoes. If you need to take a kid's shoes to stop him from running away, that kid needs to be in residential treatment.

I had a client whose mom found a Tupperware container of her daughter's razor blades, which she was using to cut herself. When the mom confiscated it, the daughter had a temper tantrum, and the mom ended up giving them back to her. She rationalized it by telling me, "I thought if I didn't give it back, then she'd use something else that she isn't familiar with, and she'd really hurt herself." The moment the words left her mouth, she realized how crazy they sounded. However, in the moment, she felt she was choosing the best option available.

I understand the desire to go to extremes to protect your kid, but if you rationalize your behavior by saying, "I'm not going to let her die," that's a clear indication that it's time to put her in the hospital or in treatment.

LEGACY BEHAVIORS

There are the things we do as parents to stop our kids from falling behind, and then there are the things we do to help them get ahead. These are often referred to in psychiatry as "legacy behaviors," and it's definitely something I've been guilty of.

I remember the night my eighth-grade son came to me and announced that his science fair project was due the next day. Apparently, he'd had eight weeks to put together a report and a display board, but he hadn't even settled on a topic.

The urgency of the situation snapped me into action. I'm a doctor. I can write a research paper. So naturally, I told him, "You start printing and cutting out pictures from the Internet. Make the board. I'll start writing the report."

My efforts to rescue him ended up working out *too* well. His project was chosen for entry in the city-wide science fair, where it won first prize. He was applauded by teachers and the principal. He even got out of class to attend the fair. I had to remind him to read the report because he'd definitely get asked questions about it. I realized that I hadn't done him any favors by winning him that award. It would be a shame if the only thing he learned from science class that year is that he can succeed without doing any work.

It's hard to contemplate that your kid might end up failing, especially at a point in their life when failure may very well mean fewer options in their life, at least in the short term. But these are consequences they must learn for themselves.

I can see you thinking, "Let my kid fail out of class/high school/college? Over my dead body. I'm going to make sure their work gets done, even if I have to do it myself. That is not happening."

You can do their homework, write their essays, call them each morning to make sure they show up for class. And, hey, maybe they will get through college. At that point, what happens? Are you going to set up job interviews for them? Call them every morning to make sure they go to work? At what point will they be allowed to take responsibility for themselves?

I often have to explain to parents that as scary as it is to contemplate their child failing, it is actually much worse for their kids to never fail. Without failure, they don't understand consequences.

> I often have to explain this to kids, as well. After all, they've been spoon-fed fears about failure their whole lives. I had one girl say to me, "If I don't get into a good college, I won't get a good career." I said, "Whoa! You're fifteen years old. What does that even mean for you? What is a good life, anyway? What's a good career?" She didn't even know—it was just what she'd been taught to believe.

Even more important than academic or career success is for kids to develop personal agency, confidence, and self-esteem. This doesn't mean standing by in silence while your kid flounders. If he's struggling in school, figure out why. Get him involved in tutoring. Have him tested for learning disabilities. Get involved with his life to teach him organizational skills, time management, prioritization, and other adult techniques for functioning independently. Yes, it's a lot easier and less time-consuming to get him a prescription for Adderall, or call his teacher and ask for special accommodations. But that's not a sustainable model for parenting or your kid's life in the long term.

That's why bailing them out as teenagers is a bad idea.

To shift legacy behavior, parents need to confront the fact that the consequences they fear might not be so dire. The younger your child is, the less severe the consequences are for making mistakes. The consequences of failure for younger kids are mainly psychological. They find out what it feels like to be embarrassed, disappointed, or fall short of their own expectations. They are then able to connect the dots from those feelings to their own choices. Those feelings don't hold them back in life. Despite the dire sound of "fail," the truth is that in lower grades, most schools will still pass a kid and move him through the school system, whether he finishes his homework or not. However, once the kid is a junior in high school and has college applications due, the consequences become more of a problem.

If a kid misses college application deadlines one year, they can apply the following year. Personally, I think most kids would benefit from taking a gap year and having time to figure out what they want to do. However, parents think, "No, they have to do it exactly the way I did it," or "They have to stay on track with the four-year plan their counselor set out for them."

I know a lot of therapists who focus all their efforts on building a kid's self-esteem. But self-esteem can't be developed in a vacuum—there's no treatment protocol or manual that can make a person feel better about themselves. A kid's self-esteem comes from the things they do themselves, not the things you achieve for them. Robbing them of the opportunity to make choices for themselves is robbing them of the confidence you want them to have.

Try your new regimen for 30 days, then reassess. If it didn't work for your household, revise it. However, don't make revisions the first day, while your kids are still in revolt. Give it a good period of time before deciding if it works. Then consider whether it works. (And remember, it's not just about whether it works for *you*.)

CHAPTER SIX

CO-PARENTING

———

A few years ago, my son received some money from my mom, and he wanted to buy a car with it. Specifically, he wanted to buy a Mercedes. The car was used, but buying it would still require him to take out a five-year loan. To me, it made no sense to make that kind of financial commitment on something that was going to depreciate. When he needed someone to co-sign the loan, I said, "I'm not doing that."

He ended up asking his dad, my ex-husband, for the same favor. To his credit, his dad did give our son the same advice I had. "Lease a car," he said. "The payments will be cheaper, and the car won't depreciate on you. Keep the money from your grandma and invest it instead." But in the end, true to form, his loving but highly enabling dad went ahead and co-signed the loan so our son could get the car he wanted.

Today, my son regrets his decision. The car isn't worth what he paid for it, and that's not even counting the taxes. Whether he keeps the car or sells it, my son is going to lose money on this decision. But it was a lesson he had to learn himself.

Even when your kid is an adult, it's hard to deny them something they want. It was a hard choice for me to refuse him. I could have rationalized that he had a good job, and he had the money. Why shouldn't I support his decision? But I chose to take the long-term view. I didn't want to be the one he came back to, asking, "Why did you let me do that?"

This wasn't a huge conflict or a moral dilemma; it was a small thing. At the same time, it involved consequences for my son, and also consequences for me. Was I going to resent my son's dad being the "cool" parent? Was I going to change my mind so that my son wouldn't prefer his dad to me? Or was I going to make what I saw as the best decision and stick with it, regardless of the potential backlash?

I remember once complaining to my son's father about our kids' snacking habits. I bought fruit for them, but they would never eat it.

He said, "They eat it at my house."

I asked my kids, "Why don't you eat fruit at my house? You eat it at your dad's, right?"

They said, "Well, he cuts it up and brings it to us."

I considered this for a minute. Then I thought, well, I guess they won't be eating fruit at my house, because I'm not going to do that for them. I want them to be independent and make good choices on their own. It is also not realistic to think that their dad will stop cutting up their fruit and serving it to them.

Again, I could let this bother me. I could also have given in, and started cutting up fruit for them myself. But I chose not to do either of those things. I want what I see as the best for my kids, but the world isn't going to fall apart if they don't follow the best nutrition guidelines, get their teeth cleaned every year, or make what I think are the best decisions around how they spend their money. It's much more beneficial to my children if I put my efforts into co-parenting well with their dad.

Even minor situations like these can make or break your success in co-parenting. It's an issue I'm passionate about, because I have seen how much harm is caused for the kids when their parents can't work together effectively.

HOW TO HANDLE CO-PARENTING WELL

Most people think about the importance of co-parenting when a couple is divorced. While it is critical to co-parent cooperatively when you are divorced, it's just as important when you are still married. Not all married couples are always on the same page. (Shocking, I know.) So even if you are in a loving, committed relationship with your child's other parent, don't skip over this chapter.

Co-parenting is essentially any two people that are sharing the task of raising a child. It could be two moms, or a father and a grandparent, or any combination.

Let's face it: kids are really good at splitting parents apart when it benefits them. They know which parent to ask to get something they want, and how to pit one parent against the other to weaken the boundaries you've set for them. Successful co-parenting requires putting your differences aside for the benefit of your child, and making your kid's best interest a shared priority in your relationship. Learning how to do this will make your child feel secure, as well as teach them how to cooperate and have healthy relationships.

REDEFINE YOUR RELATIONSHIP

It probably won't surprise you that the number one thing you can do as a co-parent is get along with each other. I know it can be hard to do this, especially if you're still dealing with the hurt from whatever caused your divorce. But as a co-parenting couple, you need to make it your goal to separate your personal relationship from your parenting relationship.

It helps immensely to begin by redefining your relationship. For instance, instead of calling your ex-husband "my ex," you can refer to him as "my sons' father." Using a different term can reframe the way you see the relationship and draw the sting out of the situation.

Since you married the other person, your values are probably not too far apart from theirs. There will always be differences, but not extreme ones. If you put your anger and resentment in the back seat, make your kids a priority, and choose to cooperate for the benefit of your children, you can be successful.

The reality is that co-parenting can be an issue even for people who are still married. After all, kids know which parents are going to give in to what. The same is true for kids whose parents are divorced. They know whom to ask for rides, whom to ask for money, and whom to ask if they can stay out later. Maintaining consistency between the two parents prevents problems.

I've had multiple moms (as well as dads) say, "My kids don't want to go stay with their dad."

I usually say, "Yeah, because he has rules and structure, and you don't."

One parent generally gives in more than the other, and is more of an enabler. They always know who they are. If you're that parent, raise your hand high and say, "Yep, that's me." Now, when you feel yourself giving in, say, "You know what? I need to ask your mom before I decide." That way, you and your co-parent can try to find a middle ground.

It's not uncommon to see kids being raised in two different households with two different sets of rules. That in itself isn't a damaging form of inconsistency. If the parents can respect each other's differences, they can come up with a baseline of shared rules and standards, and support each other in enforcing the consequences when those rules get broken.

CONSISTENCY AFTER DIVORCE

After divorce, it's completely normal to have unresolved or negative feelings about your former spouse. Marriages don't usually end on perfectly amicable terms. However, it is possible to get past these feelings where it comes to your kid's well-being. I've seen scenarios in which divorced parents spend time together with their kids on holidays, at weddings, and/or when the grandkids get together. If this works for your family, great. However, if you're not at a point where you can sit across a family dinner table with your ex, that's okay too. Being overly amicable isn't always better for your kids. In fact, it can confuse them.

It's important to set a clear boundary that you are no longer married, but that you are still a united front in parenting your child. After all, your relationship as co-parents will never end. The intertwining of your lives will go on forever. That's why it's good to demonstrate that you can be friendly to each other and work as a team. When you're doing family therapy with a kid living in both homes, you need to come together for sessions. If a kid's therapist recommends a medication that one parent agrees with but the other doesn't, you have to discuss it cooperatively and come together to support each other anyway. If your kid wants your permission for something, you need to take the time to check with the kid's other parent and respect their opinion. You may not be a "we" in terms of your relationship, but your child needs to hear from both of you as "we."

When you co-parent well, your kids are more secure and confident. They don't have to deal with the stress of your relationship's conflict. A twenty-five-year study by Judith Wallerstein on the legacy of divorce found that, in a good scenario, kids have a two-year adjustment period after a divorce. In fact, if the marriage involved significant conflict, the kids actually are emotionally better off after the divorce and adjustment period.

There is no better example you can set for your kids than cooperating with your ex. Getting along with your ex means you're a bigger person. You're setting an example that even though relationships end, you can still care about someone. That example will help your kid build stronger relationships while also making him or her emotionally and mentally healthier.

GIVE UP THE POWER STRUGGLE

A startling number of parents don't want to partner with their exes in creating consistency, even when it affects their child's well-being. This always baffles me. This is twenty-first-century America, after all—nobody forced any of these parents to marry each other or have a baby with them.

Always remember that while you got to choose your co-parent, your child didn't have a say in who their parents would be. They are stuck with the parents they have, and they are programmed to love you both, even with your flaws. It's not at all fair to make your child choose between the two of you, or try to make them turn away from their other parent.

Nevertheless, I see parents do this all the time. They engage in a power struggle with the kid at the center, each trying to take out their anger at the other in distinct ways.

For men, this usually looks like trying to hold on to some bit of control in their family. It's understandable why they'd feel this way. Men are not very good at adjusting to the sense of failure that comes with divorce. In addition, when it comes to matters of custody, courts tend to favor women over men, so the man feels disadvantaged in the process of holding on to his rights as a parent (again, something he's probably not very used to feeling).

Women, on the other hand, tend toward extreme bitterness for how they've been hurt by their marriages ending. I've witnessed dozens of mothers still angry about how their ex-husbands hurt or disappointed them retaliate by turning their kids against him.

During one of my recent family therapy sessions, a mother turned to her child and said in response to a question he'd asked, "Your father had an affair."

As a therapist, I found this to be very counterproductive for both the session and the child we were all there to help, and later, I asked the mother about it. She excused herself by saying that it was the truthful answer to a question the child had asked—"I didn't want to lie."

I told her, "If you don't want to lie, don't lie, but don't vent. If the child is asking questions about what happened in your married life, you can simply say, 'What went on in our relationship is not something you need to know.'"

Honestly, though, I suspected the mother's actions had less to do with not lying to her child, and more to do with relieving her own feelings. That mom wanted to hurt the dad; instead, though, she hurt her kid.

Like I said, turning dad into a villain is a commonplace tactic for divorced mothers in the power struggle over their children. Once, a mom told me that her daughter hadn't seen her father in years. When I asked why, she answered, "He was abusive. He doesn't have any rights."

I asked, "Can I see a court order?"

"Well, no," she said. "We never did that. There's no court order." I told her I intended to contact the father, since the issues for which I was treating her daughter were greatly exacerbated by not having her dad in her life.

As soon as I called the dad, he flew down from San Francisco to meet with me. He was a very sweet, kind-hearted man who was eager to repair the relationship with his daughter to whatever extent he could. It wasn't easy, though, since the mom had been feeding the daughter a story for years that her father was a villain.

Not all moms are this deliberate or systematic about turning their children against their former spouses. Sometimes these mothers' stories about their children's fathers simply come through complaining and making negative statements about them. I remember my mom complaining, "Your dad never pays me any child support." While there might have been money issues between them, the reality was that my dad, like my mom, was doing the best he could for us. She could have talked to her therapist, her friends, or her extended family about these issues. Instead, she chose to cause my sister and me to suffer more as we took on her feelings about our father and her worries about money.

It's no wonder that, in the world of psychology, custody evaluations yield both the highest pay rates and the highest malpractice rates. Meanwhile, divorce attorneys make a fortune in this emotionally driven process. The more the parents fight, the more money is made by everyone involved in arbitrating the dispute.

It's worth noting that the Wallerstein study referenced earlier showed that, along with conflict, change in socioeconomic status caused the most harm to a kid's ability to adjust to and heal from divorce. For example, if their parents sell the family home and move into apartments, or if they have to transfer from private to public school, the kid will be negatively affected. One great way to avoid this negative impact? Don't give all your money to attorneys—instead, focus your energy on finding ways to positively co-parent.

Parents say they'll do anything for their kids. If this is true of you, don't argue in front of them, don't vent to your kids about the other parent, and don't use your kids as messengers to communicate your displeasure to the other parent. Always go straight to the other parent with any problems you have. Your co-parenting has to be about your child's future well-being, not about you.

Remember, too, that even if you're successful in turning your kid against the other parent, it's not necessarily a "win" for you. If you cut off the kid's communication with their dad, do you want your kid to do the same toward you if they feel you've hurt or offended them? If you constantly talk the other person down for having let you down or for their personal issues, what does that teach your kid about relationships? How far do you want the dysfunction to go?

Of course, there are situations in which a parent's presence is objectively bad for a child's well-being. One obvious example would be if there is abuse or chemical dependency in the picture. Another example is if a parent is neglecting their children's health and safety. In such cases, however, there should be a court order in place to limit the other parent's access based on his or her behavior. There shouldn't be any need to bring the kid into it. Think about it—what good does it do your child to tell them, "We can't afford that, because your dad hasn't paid child support this month," or "You mom just spoils you?" How do you think hearing such comments will affect your kid?

THE IMPACT OF POOR CO-PARENTING

I remember seeing a Facebook poll that asked people to choose which they'd prefer: a year in jail or another year married to their ex. A good percentage of people chose jail. How do people get to a place where they hate someone so much? In my opinion, it has everything to do with our expectations going in. When the person you love doesn't meet your expectations, it can create deep, long-lasting resentment.

It's normal to feel disappointed when your expectations aren't met. Still, those were and are your expectations to manage. For example, if you went into your marriage believing that you were going to change your spouse, that's an issue you have to work out without wrapping your kid up in it. They are likely already aware of their other parent's shortcomings (as well as yours). They don't need the added baggage of your bitterness and resentment. What they need is help navigating the relationship in spite of those shortcomings.

A mom recently tried to explain her fraught relationship with her ex by saying, "You know, my husband is really difficult."

I countered, "I don't even need to know him to tell you that he's always been difficult. That didn't change. What changed is that it's not okay with you anymore."

A kid shouldn't have to suffer for their parents' lack of ability to manage their own emotions or expectations. Rather, as the ones choosing to divorce, the parents should be the ones making sacrifices to minimize the child's suffering during the transition. A divorced dad may need to shift his finances to make sure his kids can stay in the same house and keep attending the same school. A divorced mom may need to give up her free time for a job that will help support her kids. But one of the biggest gifts that divorced parents can give their children is learning how to forgive each other.

We've all heard this before, but it bears repeating: when you don't forgive someone, it hurts you more than them. You are the one who has to live with that negative energy in your body. If you can say, "You know what? I changed my mind," taking personal responsibility instead of assigning blame, you will find a more peaceful place. It's important to own your part in what happened.

The big events that blow up a marriage—infidelity, conflict, lack of intimacy, are rarely the reason for the divorce. In fact, they are usually the result of issues that were around for a long time. If you were emotionally distant, it did not give your spouse the right to cheat, but it did contribute to their motivation.

As hard as it might be for you, you have to continue to work on your relationship with your ex in order to successfully co-parent your child. If you keep the same relationship dynamic, you'll only prolong the conflict. I know you are thinking that you left the relationship not to have to deal with them anymore, but remember, you chose to have a family with them. When you have a child with someone, your relationship with that person is never completely over. You can get them out of your house, but you can never get them out of your life.

With that in mind, a good place to start changing the relationship is being open to compromise. Nothing has to be 100 percent the way you want. Be open to your co-parent's input and have a collaborative conversation.

For instance, it's not co-parenting if you say, "I want to take our son on a tour of potential colleges, and I want you to pay for it." Instead, explain your reasoning. "I want to make sure our son gets a chance to see a few universities before he makes his choice. What are some options?"

If your co-parent turns you down, start asking questions. "Okay, what do you think would be a good way for our kid to make a decision about schools?" Don't assume that your ex does (or should) share your values or priorities. For example, my ex-husband doesn't value college the way I do. He's a chef now, so having his kids go to college wasn't important to him. He didn't contribute to that process for them. When I was a single mom, I didn't have the money to go on tours. So, I told my son, "Wait until your acceptance letters arrive and pick your top three choices. We'll look at those." I was the one who had to help him apply for student loans and take out some of my own. That was a decision I had to make on my own, because I was the parent who felt college was essential. I had to do the hard work of accepting that not sharing that value didn't make my ex-husband a bad parent. I couldn't make him want what I wanted.

Being resentful doesn't do anyone any good. You can't get mad because different things are important to your ex-spouse. You'll never find a parenting book that says, "Good parents always pay for college/buy the kid a car/ get braces, etc." Good parents love their children, support them, teach them, and do their best to make sure they have consistency in their lives. Everything else is a matter of personal preference.

It's important to acknowledge this. It will help you stay flexible, so that you and your co-parent can make decisions in the best interest of your child.

KIDS NEED THEIR DADS

While most men recognize that a child needs their mother, I've found that few women recognize the same about fathers. I've never seen a dad attempt to fully remove the mother of his child from that child's life. They may often want to control her, but they seldom want to eliminate her from the child's life.

On the other hand, I've witnessed many women take out their anger on their ex-husbands by trying to keep their children from them. What they don't realize is that they are actually hurting their child. They also tend to deeply resent a father's efforts to get back into their child's life by offering gifts and special privileges. When a dad takes a kid to Disneyland or buys him a new laptop, a mom might say something like "How lucky for him that he gets to take you on that trip. I don't have the money for it," instead of "I'm so glad you got to experience that with your dad."

Moms need to know that it's not only destructive to the child to keep them away from their dads, but it's ultimately very destructive to themselves. In keeping her child from their father, the mom is making her kid's life harder, which in turn makes her life harder. Moreover, when kids see their parents interacting in an unhealthy way, they end up doing the same with their spouses and kids.

You can't eliminate a parent from a child's life, even if it's truly impossible for the child to see them. My mom passed away, but she's still my mom and always will be. By the same token, you can keep a kid away from their dad, but he will always be their father.

Remember the mom who was addicted to painkillers from Chapter 5? When she went into treatment for her addiction, the dad told me, "She's going to call and ask to borrow $50,000. I just know it. She's going to make me pay for her treatment."

I said, "And you're going to do it, because that will be the best fifty grand you've ever spent. That's your child's mother. She's sick, and she needs help. You're going to do it so that someday your kids will know you were there for their mom, not because you loved her, but because you loved them."

He got very quiet. It had never crossed his mind that the way he treated his children's mother would affect his relationship with them, for good or for bad.

As kids grow up, they come to realize the strengths and weaknesses of each parent for themselves. They'll clearly see whether or not their dad was willing to help their mom the way he should have, or if their mom let them get away with more than she should have. They can look back and evaluate things accurately: "You know, it was really weird how my mom was struggling to pay the bills while my dad took me to Disneyland." The gifts, vacations, and other grand gestures won't mean much in the long run. What will matter is how the parents contributed to their children's well-being. A big part of that is the level of respect with which parents treat each other.

No matter what kids say, they ultimately love both of their parents. They love your ex, and they love you. If they hear you saying mean things about their other parent, you can imagine the conflict they feel inside. This conflict is the hardest part of a child's healing from and adjusting to divorce. Don't make it harder for them through bitterness, negative talk, and vindictive actions.

My stepdaughter once told me that she did not know how to have a relationship with both of her parents at the same time. One time, while she was making a birthday card for her dad, her mom walked in. My stepdaughter told me that when her mom saw what she was doing, she reacted with bitterness, saying, "I didn't need to see that."

The daughter answered, "You taught me to be respectful." That was a great response, but the child shouldn't have had to justify making her father a card. Her mom should have found something positive to say, like, "That's thoughtful of you." Saying nothing at all would have been better than making a remark that casts the child's love for her father in a negative light.

When an issue arises between you and your co-parent, check-in with yourself. Ask, "Is this about my frustrations and disappointment with the marriage? Or is it about parenting our child well?" Find that pause button so that you can lose the reactivity and recover some self-awareness.

Remember that when you communicate with your ex, your purpose is to ensure your child's well-being. Keep a neutral tone and make requests rather than demands. Listen to your co-parent to try to figure out what's really at stake. Instead of shutting them down right away, treat your ex with respect. Be careful not to let the conversation digress into your own needs. Instead, keep the focus on the issue you're trying to resolve.

For small differences in parenting, just let them happen. It's not a big deal that my boys' dad cut up fruit for the them. I just thought, "Okay. At least they're eating fruit at their dad's." Just stick to your own boundaries. Don't give in out of fear that your kids will like the other parent more. In the long term, your kids will respect you more if you maintain consistency, both in your own actions and in how you act toward your ex.

No parents build their post-divorce relationship perfectly.

Even in the best scenario, each has moments when they are furious with the other. Divorce is always difficult. The huge emotions involved mean there is always conflict at first. But once the emotions calm down, it's easier to figure the new relationship out, to forgive your ex (as well as yourself), and move on to make better choices.

Remember, when your kid hits a milestone, the only person as excited as you are is your co-parent. Similarly, when a child is suffering, the only other person who will care as much as the mom is the dad. Whether your kid gets into Yale or flunks out of school, it's invaluable to support each other through parenting's highs and lows.

CHAPTER SEVEN

GETTING HELP

—

A fellow therapist and friend of mine told me about an incident that happened with her nineteen-year-old son, who was living at home while attending a local college. He was smoking in his room in defiance of the rules she'd clearly set out for him while he was living at her house. He thought he had a pretty smart plan—running a fan that would blow the weed smoke out the window—but as the smoke drifted out, it descended directly in front of the kitchen window, where his mom could smell it immediately.

When his mom asked him if he was smoking in his room, he didn't have an option except to admit it. Furious, she called her friend for advice. "I need to kick him out, right?" Her friend confirmed this. After all, the mom had told her son at the outset never to smoke in the house. So the next day, while he was at school, she packed up his stuff and dropped it off at his dad's house.

It was a hard decision for this mother to make. She worried that by pushing him out, she would actually create more of the behavior she was trying to avoid, since she wouldn't be around to monitor him. Many other moms in her social circle thought she was nuts for responding the way she did. His dad would let him do anything he wanted—she'd lose all influence over her son. She feared losing her relationship with her son forever. But this mom knew that consequences must be swift and secure. She knew it would take something drastic for her message to be heard.

Her son was indeed very mad at her. But as it turned out, even though he stayed at his dad's house for a while, he still needed his mom emotionally. Eventually, he moved back in with her, and this time respected her rules about smoking. Their relationship survived. She was afraid she would lose her kid forever by holding her boundary, but as he got older, he ended up respecting her more for it.

THE IMPORTANCE OF AN OUTSIDE PERSPECTIVE

As we've discussed at different points in this book, it takes an average of two years between a kid developing serious behavioral problems and a parent actually reaching out for help with those problems. During those years, matters become progressively worse as parents either hope their child's behavioral problems will go away or try to deal with them themselves.

By the time the family comes into my treatment, they're sick. They've been living in a state of sympathetic arousal. For too long, they've been walking on eggshells and living in fear of the future. Then, when they come to treatment, they no longer have the stamina to see it through. It would be so much better if those parents reached out for help as soon as they knew something was wrong.

The thing is, "getting help" doesn't always mean putting your kid into treatment or even going to a therapist yourself. It can be as simple as reaching out to someone trustworthy for support.

As a parent, you are too close to your kid's problem to help with it. You are reacting from fear. You'll end up saying, "I don't want them to fall behind in school, so I'm doing their homework for them." Or, "They'll be angry if I get them help, so I won't." You stop noticing or even caring whether you're making bad decisions, because you'll feel like you're saving your child's life.

That's why you need the support of someone who is not as involved, someone who won't be manipulated by the kid or their fears about him or her.

Recently, a girl in session with me told her mom, "If I have to do this, I'm not going to be able to go to school or get my homework done." She was attempting to manipulate her mom, saying something that she knew would create fear that something that was important to the mom wouldn't happen. If that girl had been doing that kind of bullying on an ongoing basis for a long period of time, there was no chance her mom still had the emotional resources to manage it. But as an outsider to their relationship, I could clearly see the bullying and had no fear of telling the girl in that moment, "You're totally manipulating your mother."

Another time, a client of mine told his mother he would kill himself if she didn't turn the Internet back on. I said to the mom, "What, are you going to buy him a BMW, too? At what point do you stop? I'd use that threat too, if it worked. If he is going to kill himself, take him to the hospital and have him assessed. But whatever you do, don't give him the Internet."

Parenting from fear frequently feels worried and anxious. Parenting from love trusts that your children are good and want to do good, and feel good. Parenting from fear doesn't let your children solve their own problems. Parenting from love understands they need to work things out on their own, and that failure is part of learning. Parenting from fear insists on perfect grades, performance in everything. Parenting from love accepts children where they are and helps them where they need help. Parenting from fear, you can't handle your child's emotion or your own difficult emotion—they're not acceptable. Parenting from love understands that as humans, we feel everything on the spectrum, and it's not personal.

There's no way around it—child-rearing is hard work. It's especially hard when you're in a place of enabling and codependency, a parenting approach that revolves around "I'm okay if you are." When the child's life revolves around destructive behavior, and the family revolves around the child, the destructive behavior becomes the center of the entire home.

No family plans to end up in this destructive cycle. It happens over time, as parents gradually lose perspective on the situation.

One of my clients was a girl whose father had become utterly unable to set limits for her. She constantly overspent on the credit cards he gave her, and I told him to cancel the cards. He told me he'd done it, but the girl was getting packages delivered to her while she was in treatment.

When I confronted the dad about this, he broke down. He had lost his son to a drug overdose, and he had only his daughter now. He was terrified of doing anything that might turn her against him. One time, in a session with both of them, the girl accused us both of keeping her locked up. I pointed at the door. "The door's open," I said. "You can walk out anytime." The dad looked at me with a horrified expression. Losing her was his worst fear—he couldn't bear the idea of it. The threats were so real for him; he had already lost one kid. They were so real that he was unable to let go. He pulled her from treatment.

They say only your parents can love you to death. Parents like that dad can't recognize that they're enabling the very behavior that will end up making their worst fear a reality. By giving into his daughter out of fear, he was preventing her long-term success.

Parents do crazy things out of fear. They're not bad parents—they're just too deeply involved. In the moment, it can seem logical to drive your kid to pick up his drugs, or give her back her carton of razor blades, or pull him out of treatment.

There was one woman I met whose daughter had misophonia, a disorder that meant she couldn't hear certain sounds without experiencing distress. Her mom's voice was one of them, so her mom took phone calls in the garage. Another trigger was chewing, so the whole family blended their food.

Again, parents don't get to this level overnight. When a kid has issues, the insanity slowly builds in the family, their willingness to overlook bad behavior inching closer and closer toward craziness until one day, crazy is the new normal. If you don't get support to help you maintain perspective and make the right decisions in the early stages of the behavior, you'll enter into a pattern of fear-based parenting. At the point where you are unable to break that pattern, the only recourse is to seek professional help.

ADDRESSING THE PROBLEM RIGHT AWAY

Psychiatrist John Gottman, who has been studying divorce for twenty-five years, worked with his wife to put together a four-step plan for processing arguments. In the process, the arguers talk about how they felt and what triggered them, and then they share past events that might relate to these feelings. The goal of the process isn't to convert the other person to your way of thinking, but to find mutual understanding.

The process is designed for couples, but I use it with families all the time. If a parent and child have a fight, I tell them to come to therapy so we can go through it. It's amazing what can happen when the kids and parents share their perspectives with the goal of understanding each other instead of trying to change each other.

Once, I was working with a girl who had been in the foster system before being adopted. She had broken some rules at home, so her mom had kicked her out, and she was living with a friend. She let her friend use her debit card, and then it got hacked.

When the girl called her mom, who was a co-signer on her bank account, her mom said, "I have to cancel the card." The girl lost it, and they got into a huge fight. I had them come in for a session. Each of them shared their perspective, and the girl explained that when she heard her mom was going to cancel the debit card, she heard, "I'm taking your food away."

I asked the girl to say more about what feeling or memory that idea brought up for her. She explained that on her eighth birthday, she was in a foster home, and her foster sister wouldn't let her eat her birthday cake. She started sobbing. That was what triggered the fight, and, by hearing it, her mom was able to understand the anger.

Then the mom shared her perspective. She'd had a relationship with someone who ended up leaving her with a bunch of back taxes, and it took her a while to get out of that debt. Now, she said, she felt like she was being placed back under a financial threat.

After this process, the foster mother and daughter

understood each other. They didn't need to agree. They just needed to see what was important to each of them and why.

This process works best when the conflict is captured and addressed immediately. (Gottman's rule of thumb is "No sooner than 20 minutes, and no longer than 24 hours.") It's a lot easier to bring out underlying causes while the emotions are still present. When a fight happened in the past, people only remember that they had a fight, not what the fight was about. When people are in a state of sympathetic arousal, their memory ability decreases. They don't remember things when they're in fight-or-flight mode.

When a significant problem with your kid comes up, don't wait a week to address it. Seek out help that day and go through it—while the feelings and issues are still fresh in everyone's mind.

BRINGING KIDS TO THERAPY

Parents often know their kid needs therapy well before they bring them in. When they call me for an initial consultation, they often say, "I don't know how I'm going to get them there." Ultimately, though, the kids are struggling too. For the most part, they're not happy with their lives either. If they have depression and anxiety, they want to feel better.

At the same time, kids tend to be even less ready to admit they need help than their parents are. I've had kids demand an account of how my treatment program is going to help them. I've seen them do everything they can think of to manipulate their parents into pulling them out or, at the very least, pick them up early. One girl texted her mom, "If you don't come and get me, I'm going to run out of here and go play in traffic." Kids might say they're not comfortable with the staff or that they're encountering bad influences in the other program participants. I even had one kid who told his parents we didn't feed him. If the kids don't want to be there, they'll do and say anything.

In the end, lots of kids end up loving the program and everything they learn from it. At the same time, it's important for everyone in the family to know that recovery isn't linear. As with physical health, there are times during the course of therapy when a kid will feel better, and times when they'll feel worse, worse, and worse.

Remember the Cognitive Triad—our behaviors and thoughts influence our feelings, and vice versa. Recovery requires working constantly on ourselves to build and maintain mental health. Your kid might not always be in therapy, but she will always be taking care of herself in some way. Imagine being on a diet and doing really well. After three weeks, you eat a donut. You're not back where you started. You just had a dip. Similarly, if a kid has made it three weeks without smoking weed, then they smoke weed once and stop again, they're not back to where they started. They still have all the tools they learned.

At the beginning of treatment, parents have wildly varying states of mind. If parents have been dealing with these problems for years, it's likely they're not in a good emotional place.

Some parents bring their kid to therapy out of anger. To these parents, treatment is a form of punishment. Some parents are just exhausted, thinking, "I'm done with this kid," and others are paralyzed with fear that something bad might happen to their kid if they aren't there to supervise.

Generally, nearly all of the parents I encounter feel a sense of defeat, like they're throwing in the towel. They feel helpless and hopeless, angry, and scared. Most of all, they tend to ask themselves, "Am I making the right decision?"

I need to explain to all these parents, as well as their kids, that treatment is a privilege, not a punishment. There are many kids who would love treatment but can't access it. In a way, it's like tutoring. A tutor isn't punishing kids for being stupid; rather, she's providing the privilege of extra support.

Family therapy must be separate from individual therapy. In other words, the family therapist shouldn't also provide individual or couples therapy for the parents. For one thing, doing so creates a danger of aligning more with one side than the other. A kid might not feel comfortable disclosing information to a therapist who is seeing other family members.

As we discussed in Chapter Five, individual or couple's therapy is often a necessary way for parents to work out their personal issues in order to support their child's recovery. Those issues can't be the focus of family therapy, however—family therapy must focus on how the whole system operates together and how each interaction affects everyone. If family therapy becomes about one dominating theme, I recommend shifting to individual treatment.

THE TREATMENT PROCESS

To have a diagnosable condition, a kid must have an impairment in one or more areas of life, such as interpersonal relationships, school, work, or following the law. Whatever the impairments are, they cause a kid to function below the expected level for their age. Addressing these impairments is like climbing the rungs of a ladder.

ORIENTATION to TREATMENT

UTAH
IP
RTC
PHP
IOP
OP
SCHOOL COUNSELOR

Treatment begins at a low level of intervention, usually with a school counselor who is called upon to address some trouble the kid has been getting into. When questioned about the behavior, the kid might reveal a deeper issue to the counselor, such as self-harm or drug use. Or the behavior might simply continue and intensify over time, despite the counselor's repeated interventions. At that point, the counselor would admit that the situation is more than they are equipped to manage and recommend that the kid see an outpatient therapist.

If the behavior continues after the kid is involved with outpatient therapy, that therapist should recommend intensive outpatient therapy, the next rung of the ladder. This is a program that generally involves three-hour sessions three days a week. The kid may improve in that environment, or he may continue to worsen, refusing to attend school, isolating himself, becoming more depressed. This indicates a need for structure, so the kid would go to the next rung: day treatment, also called partial hospitalization, which is a six-hour-a-day, five-days-a-week therapeutic group.

From there, the next rung of treatment is residential, a seven-day-a-week program that should run for a minimum of forty-five days. While in residential treatment, a kid is provided with structure and supervision, creating an enforced "break" from their bad behavior.

From residential, the ladder goes next to hospitalization, which is less about treatment and more about stabilization. This is an important distinction to make. Some parents equate their kid being in the hospital for a week with having a week of treatment. That's not true. While there might be group therapy or other recovery-oriented activities during a hospital stay, the hospital is more about protecting the kid from death or very serious injury and getting them to a point where they can begin to rehabilitate.

In the event that one of the above levels of care doesn't work, there are also military schools, wilderness programs, and therapeutic boarding schools, which take kids for nine months to a year. These options are for the kids who, like wild mustangs that need to be broken, won't comply or cooperate.

Not everyone starts at the bottom of the ladder. Some kids start by being hospitalized after an overdose or suicide attempt and work their way down. Others start with an outpatient therapist and start going up. Generally, they all need to be under someone's thumb. For sustainable gains, kids need to be in treatment for long enough for the roots to set. The best chance for a good outcome comes from a year to eighteen months on those rungs.

The amount of time each rung takes depends on the kid's behavior. Some kids will come into our outpatient program, get sent to residential, go back to outpatient, and get sent back to residential. It's not linear. It depends on which rung is found to be medically necessary.

I had one client who went to a wilderness program as a teen. Despite the camp being out in the middle of nowhere, he escaped and sneaked away. He used a Sharpie and a toothbrush to climb down into a ravine, and then he tramped through the snow and cold until he found someone's empty summer home. He broke in, changed into dry clothes, and stole a twelve-pack of Mountain Dew. Somehow, he made it back to the camp, where the program's van was parked. He found the van's spare key behind the gas tank door, stole the van, and drove it across four states before anybody caught up to him. That's the kind of kid who is suited for a long-term treatment facility. Their adolescent brain is on fire, they feel invincible, and their severe behavioral problems affect younger kids in the home.

The way to tell whether a kid needs to move up the ladder is simple: look at whether the outcomes are changing. If their behavior is unchanged or worsening, at that point, we look at providing a higher level of care.

EXPECT PUSHBACK

Much of the time, kids don't want to stop their behavior. They're having fun, especially with substance abuse, don't see a problem with what they're doing, and can rationalize it as "everybody else is doing it." They also don't want to go into their minds and deal with the bad stuff. Who does? That's not fun.

Sometimes, kids also make up their minds that therapy doesn't work. This is a decision they will often make after just a couple of sessions didn't create an instant fix.

I always warn parents in advance about the ways kids will fight, threaten, and manipulate in order to avoid therapy. I explain how kids know what's important to their parents and will use it to bully them. If education is important to a parent, the kid will say they'll fall behind in school. If the parent is concerned about finances, the kid tells them it's going to be a waste of money. If the parent's feelings are easily hurt, the kid will threaten to hate them forever or never let them see their grandchildren.

All this preparation is crucial for parents. When they get that phone call from their child, they're ready. In fact, they're often surprised at how we were able to predict the exact thing their kid would say. For many, it's a lightbulb moment—they realize their kid has been manipulating them all along, and that the only reason they couldn't see it before was because the fear was too overwhelming.

DON'T JUST READ THIS BOOK—DO SOMETHING

I've seen truly amazing results come from out of my therapeutic sessions and treatment programs: improved relationships, good communication, reconnecting in a healthy, loving family system. Some of these results took hold in the least likely circumstances.

Once, I treated a kid who became depressed when he was twelve. His parents were great, he had no trauma; it was just a chemical imbalance that showed no signs until one day when the police found the boy in a park after a botched suicide attempt.

I almost didn't want to take this kid on, he was so depressed. I did, however, and after we did some genetics testing and got him on the right medication, he was a new kid. It was miraculous to see. A few years later, his parents sent me a little video, showing him getting a driver's license, going on trips with his parents, and going to college. That kid could have died in a park without his parents being able to do anything about it on their own.

Another girl first came to me as a young adult on her fifth round of treatment. She had been in treatment for everything from eating disorders to heroin, and her parents were as close as you can get to the point of giving up. By the time she came to my program, no one held a lot of hope that this latest round was going to be successful, but her parents never gave up. They went through the hard stuff, even separating for the good of their child. As of today, the girl has been sober for years, and she runs her own treatment center.

Every parent wants results like these. But the big question is whether they want it badly enough to go through the process to get there.

As you're coming to the end of this book, consider where you're at now. Are you thinking, "Well, now that I've read this book, I don't need to get professional help"? If so, I'm sorry, but you've missed the point. That's like saying, "I went to the gym and sat on the bike for an hour, but I didn't move." This book isn't a fix—it's a series of recommendations of things you can and must do. Just reading it and not taking action is a waste of your time.

I won't sugarcoat it for you. Working your way back to a healthy family dynamic is hard. It's particularly hard when neither you nor your kid have ever taken any steps toward improving mental health. Don't expect it to be an overnight change. Going from crisis mode to something sustainable takes a long time. And after that, it takes even more time to get to a place of outstanding health.

All this said, I can promise you that when a family commits to mental health and a functional system, there are tremendous rewards that keep leading you forward. There are a hundred success stories, big and small, that you will experience along the way. By sharing in this process together, your family will heal.

CONCLUSION

As you walk away from this book, what I want most for you is to have a sense of hope. First, in knowing that you're not alone. Second, in knowing that you can't fix this any more than you can fix diabetes or any other illness. It's not your job. No one expects you to do it yourself. You can't fix the problem, but you can change how you contribute to it.

Now that you have this information, it's only as good as what you do with it. Everyone's next step will be different. Be proactive in your role as a parent. Make a list of all the things that have gone on and decide what isn't working for you anymore. Sign up for something out of your comfort zone. Most importantly, pick up the phone and contact someone who can help you move forward.

You don't have to go with the first therapist you consult. Look for someone you like and trust, and when you find them, follow their advice. They know what they're doing. Don't hire a therapist and then ignore what they tell you to do. You don't get credit just for showing up, so don't dictate treatment by saying, "I'll do this, but not that." You wouldn't do that for a serious health issue, so why would you choose to do it for a mental health issue?

Remember, this is a day-to-day lifelong struggle. You're in for a marathon, not a sprint. Nothing changes overnight, but it's not supposed to. Know that whatever presents itself, you can handle it. No matter how old your kid is or how long you've been making the wrong choices, the situation is still fixable. As a species, we have an amazing ability to change.

WAYS TO FIND MORE SUPPORT

- Al-Anon

Al-Anon was designed for someone caring for an alcoholic, a position that easily becomes co-dependent and enabling. These principles carry over naturally to dealing with mental health. I highly suggest getting involved in parent-focused Al-Anon to receive support, learn better communication with your child, and find community with other parents.

- National Association for Mental Illness (nami.org)

NAMI's motto is "You're not alone." They hold parent support meetings, offer help through local chapters, and provide a lot of online information for parents.

- ROWI Teen & Parent Wellness Center (rowiteen. com)

To learn more about the services my colleagues and I offer at ROWI, you can also check out our website. In addition to on-site therapy sessions and treatment programs, I provide remote parent coaching over the phone.

YOU'RE NOT ALONE

As parents, we make choices all day long. Some are good, and some are bad. No one will make every choice perfectly. If you make more good choices than bad ones, you're moving in the right direction. While some issues last a lifetime, and have to be managed rather than "cured," many of the struggles your child deals with are completely curable.

Your kid is for sure unique and special, but the issues they're going through aren't. They're not the first ones or the only ones to feel the way they do or have the types of struggles they do. If you related to the stories and the other parents in this book, and if you came to better understand your family's situation, I'm excited for you.

You're on your way to learning more about your kid and yourself. And the more you learn, the more empowered you will be to make the decisions that will help your family.

You can't have both fear and love at the same time. The more steps you take in the direction of parenting out of love, the less fear you'll feel. Every step helps. Each small shift creates more changes, sending you in the right direction.

ACKNOWLEDGMENTS

———

Where do I begin?

Let's start with my two sons Alex and Nick, who allowed me to conduct my original research on parenting with them, and now allow me to write about it in an effort to help others.

My husbands Hans and Greg. Thank you for being grown-ups and getting along, for being willing to be in each other's lives so that my boys don't have to choose whom to spend holidays with. (At least until they get married.)

This is dedicated to all of the exceptional clinicians whose teams I have had the privilege of being on. Each of you has made me want to be better and work harder to make a difference for all of our kiddos.

Milagros	Marni	Tsoline	Johnny
Natalie	Rachie	Jodi	Heather
Ali	George	Lexi	Lindsey
Alyse	Amanda	Rene	Courtney
Viviana	Saro	Sheila	DRB
Alison	Brittney	Kory	Janine
Karen	Natasha	Patt	Marissa

ABOUT THE AUTHOR

—

DR. CANDICE FEINBERG, Psy.D. is a licensed clinical psychologist. She is a highly respected authority in the field of mental health and addiction issues, and an industry leader in developing innovative, evidence-based therapeutic programs. She has appeared on national television, written articles published in *Psychology Today,* and spoken at conferences across the country.

Dr. Feinberg earned her doctorate at Phillips Graduate Institute. Her dissertation was *Wired Teens and their Social Development: Delineating Between Function and Addiction.* Since 2007, she has worked in adolescent treatment, combining a rare set of talents as a psychologist, consultant, teacher and administrator.

Along with guiding hundreds of families in many stages

of recovery, Dr. Feinberg pioneered a dynamic therapy program focusing on the critical role of the parent in their children's recovery. She also served on the board of For the Child, a nonprofit dedicated to providing therapeutic services in schools.

Dr. Feinberg is currently the CEO of ROWI Teen & Parent Wellness Center in Thousand Oaks, California, where she is known for her direct approach to parent coaching and "out-of-the-box" approach to treatment.